PORT AND MARITIME SECURITY

PORT AND MARITIME SECURITY

JONATHON P. VESKY
EDITOR

Nova Science Publishers, Inc.
New York

Copyright © 2008 by Nova Science Publishers, Inc.

All rights reserved. No part of this book may be reproduced, stored in a retrieval system or transmitted in any form or by any means: electronic, electrostatic, magnetic, tape, mechanical photocopying, recording or otherwise without the written permission of the Publisher.

For permission to use material from this book please contact us:
Telephone 631-231-7269; Fax 631-231-8175
Web Site: http://www.novapublishers.com

NOTICE TO THE READER
The Publisher has taken reasonable care in the preparation of this book, but makes no expressed or implied warranty of any kind and assumes no responsibility for any errors or omissions. No liability is assumed for incidental or consequential damages in connection with or arising out of information contained in this book. The Publisher shall not be liable for any special, consequential, or exemplary damages resulting, in whole or in part, from the readers' use of, or reliance upon, this material.

Independent verification should be sought for any data, advice or recommendations contained in this book. In addition, no responsibility is assumed by the publisher for any injury and/or damage to persons or property arising from any methods, products, instructions, ideas or otherwise contained in this publication.

This publication is designed to provide accurate and authoritative information with regard to the subject matter covered herein. It is sold with the clear understanding that the Publisher is not engaged in rendering legal or any other professional services. If legal or any other expert assistance is required, the services of a competent person should be sought. FROM A DECLARATION OF PARTICIPANTS JOINTLY ADOPTED BY A COMMITTEE OF THE AMERICAN BAR ASSOCIATION AND A COMMITTEE OF PUBLISHERS.

LIBRARY OF CONGRESS CATALOGING-IN-PUBLICATION DATA
Port and maritime security / Jonathan P. Vesky(editor)
    p. cm.
ISBN-13: 978-1-59454-726-3(hbk.)
ISBN-10: 1-59454-726-2(hbk.)
1. Merchant marine—Security measures—United States. 2. Harbors—Security measures—United States. 3. National Security measures—United States. 4. Civil defense—United States. 5. United States—Defenses. 6. War on Terrorism, 2001-
Vesky , Johnathon P.
VK203.P67   2008
363.12'37—dc22   2008009826

Published by Nova Science Publishers, Inc. ✢ *New York*

CONTENTS

Preface		vii
Chapter 1	Terrorist Nuclear Attacks on Seaports: Threat and Response *Jonathan Medalia*	1
Chapter 2	Port and Maritime Security: Background and Issues for Congress *John F. Frittelli*	11
Chapter 3	Maritime Security: Overview of Issues *John F. Frittelli*	43
Chapter 4	Port and Maritime Security: Potential for Terrorist Nuclear Attack Using Oil Tankers *Jonathan Medalia*	53
Index		63

PREFACE

The terrorist attacks of September 11, 2001 heightened awareness about the vulnerability to terrorist attack of all modes of transportation. Port security has emerged as a significant part of the overall debate on U.S. homeland security. The overarching issues for Congress are providing oversight on current port security programs and making or responding to proposals to improve port security. The U.S. maritime system consists of more than 300 sea and river ports with more than 3,700 cargo and passenger terminals. However, a large fraction of maritime cargo is concentrated at a few major ports. Most ships calling at U.S. ports are foreign owned with foreign crews. Container ships have been the focus of much of the attention on seaport security because they are seen as vulnerable to terrorist infiltration. More than 9 million marine containers enter U.S. ports each year. While the Bureau of Customs and Border Protection (CBP) analyzes cargo and other information to target specific shipments for closer inspection, it physically inspects only a small fraction of the containers. The Coast Guard and CBP are the federal agencies with the strongest presence in seaports. In response to September 11, 2001, the Coast Guard created the largest port-security operation since World War II. The Coast Guard has advanced its 24-hour Notice of Arrival (NOA) for ships to a 96-hour NOA. The NOA allows Coast Guard officials to select high risk ships for boarding upon their arrival at the entrance to a harbor. CBP has also advanced the timing of cargo information it receives from ocean carriers. Through the Container Security Initiative (CSI) program, CBP inspectors pre-screen U.S.-bound marine containers at foreign ports of loading. The Customs Trade Partnership Against Terrorism (C-TPAT) offers importers expedited processing of their cargo if they comply with CBP measures for securing their entire supply chain. To raise port security standards, Congress passed the Maritime Transportation Security Act of 2002 (P.L. 107-295) in November 2002. The focus of debate in Congress has been about whether current efforts to improve port security are adequate in addressing the threat. While many agree that Coast Guard and CBP programs to address the threat are sound, they contend that these programs represent only a framework for building a maritime security regime, and that significant gaps in security still remain.

Chapter 1 - A terrorist nuclear attack on a U.S. seaport could cause local devastation and affect the global economy. Terrorists might obtain a bomb in several ways, though each poses difficulties. Ability to detect a bomb appears limited. The United States is using technology, intelligence, international cooperation, etc., to try to thwart an attack. Issues for Congress include safeguarding foreign nuclear material, mitigating economic effects of an attack, and allocating funds between ports and other potential targets.

Chapter 2- The terrorist attacks of September 11, 2001 heightened awareness about the vulnerability to terrorist attack of all modes of transportation. Port security has emerged as a significant part of the overall debate on U.S. homeland security. The overarching issues for Congress are providing oversight on current port security programs and making or responding to proposals to improve port security.

The U.S. maritime system consists of more than 300 sea and river ports with more than 3,700 cargo and passenger terminals. However, a large fraction of maritime cargo is concentrated at a few major ports. Most ships calling at U.S. ports are foreign owned with foreign crews. Container ships have been the focus of much of the attention on seaport security because they are seen as vulnerable to terrorist infiltration. More than 9 million marine containers enter U.S. ports each year. While the Bureau of Customs and Border Protection (CBP) analyzes cargo and other information to target specific shipments for closer inspection, it physically inspects only a small fraction of the containers.

The Coast Guard and CBP are the federal agencies with the strongest presence in seaports. In response to September 11, 2001, the Coast Guard created the largest port-security operation since World War II. The Coast Guard has advanced its 24-hour Notice of Arrival (NOA) for ships to a 96-hour NOA. The NOA allows Coast Guard officials to select high risk ships for boarding upon their arrival at the entrance to a harbor. CBP has also advanced the timing of cargo information it receives from ocean carriers. Through the Container Security Initiative (CSI) program, CBP inspectors pre-screen U.S.-bound marine containers at foreign ports of loading. The Customs Trade Partnership Against Terrorism (C-TPAT) offers importers expedited processing of their cargo if they comply with CBP measures for securing their entire supply chain.

To raise port security standards, Congress passed the Maritime Transportation Security Act of 2002 (P.L. 107-295) in November 2002. The focus of debate in Congress has been about whether current efforts to improve port security are adequate in addressing the threat. While many agree that Coast Guard and CBP programs to address the threat are sound, they contend that these programs represent only a framework for building a maritime security regime, and that significant gaps in security still remain. The GAO has investigated how the CSI and C-TPAT programs are being implemented and found several shortcomings that need correction. The GAO found that C-TPAT participants were benefitting from reduced scrutiny of their imported cargo after they had been certified into the program but before CBP had validated that the participants were indeed carrying out the promised security measures. The GAO also found that not all containers that CBP had targeted for inspection at the overseas loading port were being inspected by the host customs administration.

Chapter 3- In the wake of the terrorist attacks of September 11, 2001, port security has emerged as a significant part of the overall debate on U.S. homeland security. Many security experts believe ports are vulnerable to terrorist attack because of their size, easy accessibility by water and land, and the tremendous amount of cargo they handle. To raise port security standards, Congress passed the Maritime Transportation Security Act of 2002 (P.L. 107-295) in November 2002. In the 108th Congress, there is growing debate about whether current efforts to improve port securityare proceeding at sufficient pace and whether the nation is devoting enough resources for this purpose.

Chapter 4- While much attention has been focused on threats to maritime security posed by cargo container ships, terrorists could also attempt to use oil tankers to stage an attack. If they were able to place an atomic bomb in a tanker and detonate it in a U.S. port, they would cause massive destruction and might halt crude oil shipments worldwide for some time. Detecting a bomb in a tanker would be difficult. Congress may consider various options to address this threat.

In: Port and Maritime Security
Editor: Jonathon P. Vesky

ISBN 1-59454-726-2
© 2008 Nova Science Publishers, Inc.

Chapter 1

TERRORIST NUCLEAR ATTACKS ON SEAPORTS: THREAT AND RESPONSE[*]

Jonathan Medalia

ABSTRACT

A terrorist nuclear attack on a U.S. seaport could cause local devastation and affect the global economy. Terrorists might obtain a bomb in several ways, though each poses difficulties. Ability to detect a bomb appears limited. The United States is using technology, intelligence, international cooperation, etc., to try to thwart an attack. Issues for Congress include safeguarding foreign nuclear material, mitigating economic effects of an attack, and allocating funds between ports and other potential targets.

BACKGROUND

Terrorists have tried to obtain weapons of mass destruction (WMD) — chemical, biological, radiological, and nuclear weapons. While it would probably be more difficult for terrorists to obtain or fabricate a nuclear weapon than other WMD, an attack using a nuclear weapon

---

[*] From CRS Report RS21293; January 24, 2005.

merits consideration because it would have much higher consequence. U.S. seaports could be targets for terrorist attack. A terrorist Hiroshima-sized nuclear bomb (15 kilotons, the equivalent of 15,000 tons of TNT) detonated in a port would destroy buildings out to a mile or two; start fires, especially in a port that handled petroleum and chemicals; spread fallout over many square miles; disrupt commerce; and kill many people. Many ports are in major cities. By one estimate, a 10- to 20-kiloton weapon detonated in a major seaport would kill 50,000 to 1 million people and would result in direct property damage of $50 to $500 billion, losses due to trade disruption of $100 billion to $200 billion, and indirect costs of $300 billion to $1.2 trillion.[1]

Terrorists might try to smuggle a bomb into a U.S. port in many ways, but containers may offer an attractive route. A container is a metal box, typically 8 ft wide by 8½ ft high by 20 ft or 40 ft long, that can be used on and moved between a tractor-trailer, a rail car, or a ship. Much global cargo moves by container. Nearly 9 million containers a year enter the United States by ship.[2] Customs and Border Protection (CBP) screens data for all containers, and reportedly inspects about 6 percent of them.[3] Containers could easily hold a nuclear weapon. Many believe that ports and containers are vulnerable. An FBI official stated, "The intelligence that we have certainly points to the ports as a key vulnerability of the United States and of a key interest to certain terrorist groups...."[4] CBP Commissioner Robert Bonner believes an attack using a nuclear bomb in a container would halt container shipments, leading to "devastating" consequences for the global economy. ..."[5] People can, however, find ways to minimize economic problems.

Terrorist Nuclear Weapons: Routes to a Bomb. A terrorist group might obtain a bomb, perhaps with the yield of the Hiroshima bomb, by several plausible routes.

Russia. Strategic (long-range) nuclear weapons are reportedly well guarded on missiles or, thanks in part to U.S. assistance, in storage. In contrast, thousands of shorter-range lower-yield weapons intended for use in combat are less well secured, and numbers and locations are uncertain. (See CRS Report RL32202, *Nuclear Weapons in Russia: Safety, Security, and Control Issues*.) A fear is that terrorists might buy or steal one of these weapons along with information on how to bypass any use-control devices.

Pakistan. U.S., British, Chinese, French, and Israeli nuclear weapons are thought to be well guarded. Control is less certain for India and Pakistan. Reports indicate that Pakistanis aided nuclear programs in Iran, Libya, and North Korea, and there are concerns about the security of Pakistani nuclear weapons if President Musharraf were assassinated.[6]

Build a Bomb. The Hiroshima bomb was a "gun assembly" weapon. Its nuclear explosive was a gun barrel about 6 inches in diameter by 6 feet long. It was capped at each end, with standard explosive at one end, a mass of uranium highly enriched in the isotope 235 (highly enriched uranium, or HEU) next to the explosive, and a second HEU mass at the other end. Detonating the explosive shot one mass of HEU into the other, rapidly assembling a mass large enough to support a fission chain reaction. (Plutonium cannot be used.) This is the simplest type of nuclear weapon. U.S. scientists had such high confidence in the design that they did not test the Hiroshima bomb. Experts agree that terrorist groups could not make special nuclear material (SNM, i.e., fissile plutonium or HEU). Many believe that a terrorist group with access to HEU and key skills could build a crude nuclear weapon. Five former Los Alamos nuclear weapons experts held that such a weapon "could be constructed by a group not previously engaged in designing or building nuclear weapons, providing a number of requirements were adequately met."[7] A National Research Council study stated: "The basic technical information needed to construct a workable nuclear device is readily available in the open literature. The primary impediment that prevents countries or technically competent terrorist groups from developing nuclear weapons is the availability of SNM, especially HEU."[8] Many believe it would be hard for a terrorist group to obtain enough HEU for a weapon; others fear that terrorists could do so. The National Research Council study rated the threat level from SNM from Russia as "High — large inventories of SNM are stored at many sites that apparently lack inventory controls and indigenous threats have increased."[9]

RESPONSES

The main approach to reducing vulnerability to a terrorist nuclear attack is defense in depth — using multiple methods to detect and interdict a weapon. It would be harder to evade several methods than one: attempts to evade one may make a bomb more visible to another or reduce the odds that the bomb would work. Defense in depth also seeks to push detection and interdiction far from U.S. shores. This section illustrates the scope of effort.

Programs to Secure Nuclear Weapons and Materials. One report saw securing "existing stockpiles of nuclear weapons and materials" as "the most critical and cost-effective step to prevent nuclear terrorism."[10] To this end, the Department of Energy (DOE) operates the Materials Protection, Control, and Accounting Program (MCP&A) to secure fissile materials in former Soviet republics, and the Department of Defense operates the Cooperative Threat Reduction Program to secure nuclear weapons there. In May 2004, DOE announced the Global Threat Reduction Initiative to secure fissile and other radioactive material worldwide.

Other International Programs. (1) The International Atomic Energy Agency has safeguards to protect, among other things, HEU in nuclear reactors. (2) A joint effort by that agency, the United States, and Russia moved HEU from a shut-down nuclear reactor in Bulgaria to Russia for conversion to a safer form of uranium.[11] (3) On May 31, 2003, President Bush announced the Proliferation Security Initiative, under which the United States and allies "have begun working on new agreements to search planes and ships carrying suspect cargo and to seize illegal weapons or missile technologies." Reports claim one such interdiction may have influenced Libya's decision to end its WMD programs.[12] (4) CBP's Container Security Initiative started in January 2002. CSI involves bilateral agreements with foreign ports that export to this nation. CBP teams work with host governments to identify high-risk containers for screening for WMD before they are loaded onto ships. CSI operated in 34 ports in January 2005.[13] (5) Under the Megaports Initiative, MCP&A provides radiation detection equipment and expertise to CBP for screening containers in foreign ports. (6) The U.N.'s International Maritime Organization promulgated the International Ship and Port Facility Security Code, effective July 1, 2004, which requires port operators, ship owners, and others to improve maritime security, such as by creating plans to respond to terrorist attack.

U.S. Domestic Programs. Various programs seek to strengthen the security of U.S. ports. As of late 2004, DHS had reportedly distributed about $560 million in port security grants in the past few years.[14] The

Maritime Transportation Security Act (MTSA) of 2002 (P.L. 107-295) requires (Sec.102) assessments of the vulnerability of vessels and U.S. maritime facilities "that may be involved in a transportation security incident," a plan for deterring and responding to such an incident, assessment of the effectiveness of antiterrorism measures at certain foreign ports, etc. CBP is implementing the Automated Commercial Environment, an electronic system to gather and analyze data on goods entering the United States to help select containers for inspection. On December 21, 2004, President Bush reportedly issued "Maritime Security Policy," National Security Presidential Directive 41/Homeland Security Presidential Directive 13. While the text has apparently not been released as of mid-January 2005, a report indicates that it requires DHS to set standards for maritime recovery operations in the event of a terrorist attack. It also requires creation of a Maritime Security Policy Coordinating Committee, development of a National Strategy for Maritime Security, integration of global maritime intelligence, coordination of domestic and international outreach, and creation of a comprehensive plan for maritime supply chain security.[15]

Enhanced Technology. The last line of defense against a terrorist nuclear attack is the ability to detect nuclear weapons or material entering the United States. A large effort is underway by government agencies, industry, and universities to develop key technologies. By one estimate, the FY2005 appropriation provides $4.1 billion for homeland security R&D.[16] Operation Safe Commerce, a Department of Transportation-CBP "program to fund business initiatives designed to enhance security for container cargo ... will provide a test-bed for new security techniques."[17] The Trade Act of 2002, P.L. 107-210, sec. 343a, mandates the establishment of a task force to "establish a program to evaluate and certify secure systems of international intermodal transport."[18]

Terrorists can counter new technologies. If the United States deploys sensors at some ports, terrorists might detonate a weapon before it is inspected, or ship it to another port. If foreign ports screened containers before being loaded onto U.S.-bound ships, terrorists could infiltrate the ports. Securing the largest ports might lead terrorists to use smaller ones. Securing every U.S.-bound container might lead terrorists to smuggle a weapon in a small boat or airplane. Detecting an HEU bomb is difficult because HEU emits very little radiation. R&D is underway to address this key issue.

In 2002 and 2003, ABC News shipped shielded 15-pound cylinders of depleted uranium (DU, natural uranium minus most uranium-235) into U.S. ports in containers. CBP did not detect these shipments. ABC claimed that DU is a good surrogate for HEU; CBP claimed the opposite. In September 2004, DHS issued a report on the topic. It concluded "[i]mprovements are needed in the inspection process to ensure that weapons of mass destruction ... do not gain access to the U.S. through oceangoing cargo containers" and recommended improving detection equipment and search methods.[19]

Pending Legislation. Bills related to terrorist nuclear attacks on ports include H.R. 163, Secure Domestic Container Partnership Act of 2005, and H.R. 173, Anti-Terrorism and Port Security Act of 2005.

POLICY ISSUES

Securing Nuclear Materials. The possibility that a terrorist group could make a nuclear weapon given enough HEU, and the difficulty of preventing terrorists from smuggling a weapon into a U.S. port, show the value of securing nuclear weapons and materials in Russia and elsewhere. Are current efforts sufficient?

Forensics. Technology may enable identification of the origin of nuclear material used in a bomb. This forensic capability strengthens the value of controlling Russian nuclear weapons and materials: finding that material for a bomb detonated in the United States came from Russia, a likely source, would in all probability lead to the conclusion that the material was stolen rather than that Russia conducted the attack. At the same time, augmenting already-excellent forensic capability through technology and intelligence could help deter other nations from giving nuclear materials to terrorists.

Ports in Major Cities. The terrorist weapons discussed earlier, while lower in yield than strategic weapons, might produce blast damage over a radius of 1 to 2 miles, and fire and fallout beyond that range. Accordingly, it might be argued that ports with the greatest number of people living or working within a mile or two of cargo docks, such as

Philadelphia and New York, should have highest priority in receiving security resources.

Ameliorating Economic Consequences. Cold War civil defense studies examined how to ameliorate the destructive effects of a large nuclear attack. This effort, and more recent emergency preparedness efforts, provide a template for response and recovery following a terrorist attack using one 15-kiloton weapon. This work does not, however, address possible global economic consequences and how to predict and mitigate them. These issues could benefit from further study and analyses.

What Priority Should Port Security Have? The 9/11 Commission wrote, "Opportunities to do harm are as great, or greater, in maritime or surface transportation [compared to commercial aviation]. Initiatives to secure shipping containers have just begun." Terrorists "may be deterred by a significant chance of failure."[20] Improving the ability to detect terrorist nuclear weapons in the maritime transportation system may make a terrorist attack on a port less likely to succeed, and thus less probable. The American Association of Port Authorities, a trade association, welcomed federal grants for port security upgrades to comply with the MTSA, but called for "substantially greater resources."[21] Others agree that more resources are needed to secure U.S. ports, such as to reduce overcrowding of cargo-handling facilities and to hire more workers.[22] A similar case could be made for gas pipelines, electric power plants, rail yards, or bridges. At issue for Congress is how to allocate security funds among ports and other potential targets.

REFERENCES

[1] ABT Associates, "The Economic Impact of Nuclear Terrorist Attacks on Freight Transport Systems in an Age of Seaport Vulnerability," executive summary, April 30, 2003, p. 7, [http://www.abtassociates.com/reports/ES-Economic_Impact_of_Nuclear_Terrorist_Attacks.pdf].

[2] U.S. Department of Homeland Security, Bureau of Customs and Border Protection, "Remarks by Commissioner Robert C.

Bonner, Council on Foreign Relations, New York, New York," January 11, 2005.
[3] Caitlin Harrington, "Post-Election Analysis: Millions of Dollars Ride on a Simple Definition of 'Inspection,'" *CQ Homeland Security,* January 7, 2005.
[4] U.S. Senate Committee on the Judiciary, Subcommittee on Technology, Terrorism, and Government Information, Hearing: "Covering the Waterfront — A Review of Seaport Security since September 11, 2001," January 27, 2004; Statement of Gary M. Bald, Acting Assistant Director Counterterrorism Division, FBI. Transcript by Federal Document Clearing House, Inc.
[5] U.S. Dept. of the Treasury, U.S. Customs Commissioner Robert Bonner, Speech Before the Center for Strategic and International Studies, Washington, D.C., January 17, 2002, [http://www.cbp.gov/xp/cgov/newsroom/commissioner/speeches_statements/archives/jan172002.xml].
[6] David Sanger and William Broad, "From Rogue Nuclear Programs, Web of Trails Leads to Pakistan," *New York Times,* Jan. 4, 2004, p. 1 and "One Man's Fortune," *Washington Post,* Dec. 27, 2003, p. 24.
[7] J. Carson Mark, Theodore Taylor, Eugene Eyster, William Maraman, and Jacob Wechsler, "Can Terrorists Build Nuclear Weapons?" Nuclear Control Institute, Washington, [http://www.nci.org/ k-m/makeab.htm]. Requirements include detailed design drawings; individuals with a wide range of weapons skills; equipment; and preparations to create a bomb quickly after obtaining HEU to reduce the risk of detection.
[8] National Research Council, Committee on Science and Technology for Countering Terrorism,*Making the Nation Safer: The Role of Science and Technology in Countering Terrorism,* Washington, National Academy Press, 2002, p. 40. [http://www.nap.edu/catalog/10415.html].
[9] Ibid., p. 44.
[10] Matthew Bunn, "Preventing Nuclear Terrorism: A Progress Update," Project on Managing the Atom, Harvard University, and Nuclear Threat Initiative, October 22, 2003, p. 4.
[11] "IAEA, USA, Russia Assist Bulgaria in Removal of HEU Fuel," staff report, International Atomic Energy Agency, December 24,

2003, at [http://www.iaea.org/NewsCenter/News/2003/Bulgaria20031224.html].

[12] Robin Wright, "Ship Incident May Have Swayed Libya," *Washington Post,* Jan.1, 2004: 19.

[13] "Remarks by Commissioner Robert C. Bonner," January 11, 2005.

[14] Sam Hananel, "Report Criticizes Use of Port Security Grants," *Washington Post,* December 29, 2004: 17.

[15] Martin Edwin Andersen, "New Bush National Security Directive on Maritime Issues Charts Administration Course During His Second Term," *Port Security News,* January 18, 2005.

[16] American Association for the Advancement of Science, "Defense and Homeland Security R&D Hit New Highs in 2005; Growth Slows for Other Agencies," November 29, 2004.

[17] U.S. Department of Homeland Security, Bureau of Customs and Border Protection. "Customs and DOT Launch 'Operation Safe Commerce' Program," November 20, 2002, p. 1.

[18] The MTSA Senior Policy Group was established in early 2004 to address mandates in MTSA and the Trade Act that DHS take steps to secure international intermodal cargo shipments. The group is led by the DHS Directorate of Border and Transportation Security and has representatives from the Department of Transportation, the Transportation Security Administration, the Coast Guard, and the Bureau of Customs and Border Protection. Information provided by Department of Homeland Security, August 17, 2004.

[19] U.S. Department of Homeland Security. Office of Inspector General. *Effectiveness of Customs and Border Protection's Procedures to Detect Uranium in Two Smuggling Incidents.* OIG-04-40, September 2004, 4 p.

[20] U.S. National Commission on Terrorist Attacks upon the United States. *The 9/11 Commission Report.* (New York: Norton, 2004), p. 391.

[21] American Association of Port Authorities, "U.S. Ports Laud Additional Federal Security Grants; Caution More Assistance Is Needed," news release, December 10, 2003, p. 1.

[22] John Broder, "At Nation's Ports, Cargo Backlog Raises Question of Security," *New York Times,* July 27, 2004: 12.

In: Port and Maritime Security
Editor: Jonathon P. Vesky

ISBN 1-59454-726-2
© 2008 Nova Science Publishers, Inc.

Chapter 2

PORT AND MARITIME SECURITY: BACKGROUND AND ISSUES FOR CONGRESS[*]

John F. Frittelli

ABSTRACT

The terrorist attacks of September 11, 2001 heightened awareness about the vulnerability to terrorist attack of all modes of transportation. Port security has emerged as a significant part of the overall debate on U.S. homeland security. The overarching issues for Congress are providing oversight on current port security programs and making or responding to proposals to improve port security.

The U.S. maritime system consists of more than 300 sea and river ports with more than 3,700 cargo and passenger terminals. However, a large fraction of maritime cargo is concentrated at a few major ports. Most ships calling at U.S. ports are foreign owned with foreign crews. Container ships have been the focus of much of the attention on seaport security because they are seen as vulnerable to terrorist infiltration. More than 9 million marine containers enter U.S. ports each year. While the Bureau of Customs and Border

---
[*] From CRS Report RL31733; May 27, 2005.

Protection (CBP) analyzes cargo and other information to target specific shipments for closer inspection, it physically inspects only a small fraction of the containers.

The Coast Guard and CBP are the federal agencies with the strongest presence in seaports. In response to September 11, 2001, the Coast Guard created the largest port-security operation since World War II. The Coast Guard has advanced its 24-hour Notice of Arrival (NOA) for ships to a 96-hour NOA. The NOA allows Coast Guard officials to select high risk ships for boarding upon their arrival at the entrance to a harbor. CBP has also advanced the timing of cargo information it receives from ocean carriers. Through the Container Security Initiative (CSI) program, CBP inspectors pre-screen U.S.-bound marine containers at foreign ports of loading. The Customs Trade Partnership Against Terrorism (C-TPAT) offers importers expedited processing of their cargo if they comply with CBP measures for securing their entire supply chain.

To raise port security standards, Congress passed the Maritime Transportation Security Act of 2002 (P.L. 107-295) in November 2002. The focus of debate in Congress has been about whether current efforts to improve port security are adequate in addressing the threat. While many agree that Coast Guard and CBP programs to address the threat are sound, they contend that these programs represent only a framework for building a maritime security regime, and that significant gaps in security still remain. The GAO has investigated how the CSI and C-TPAT programs are being implemented and found several shortcomings that need correction. The GAO found that C-TPAT participants were benefitting from reduced scrutiny of their imported cargo after they had been certified into the program but before CBP had validated that the participants were indeed carrying out the promised security measures. The GAO also found that not all containers that CBP had targeted for inspection at the overseas loading port were being inspected by the host customs administration.

INTRODUCTION

This report[1] provides background information and discusses potential issues for Congress on the topic of port security, which has emerged as a significant part of the overall debate on U.S. homeland security.[2] The terrorist attacks of September 11, 2001 heightened awareness about the vulnerability to terrorist attack of U.S. ports and the ships in them. The issue for Congress is providing oversight on port security and proposals for improving it. Port security legislation can have significant implications for public safety, the war on terrorism, the U.S. and global economy, and federal, state, and local homeland security responsibilities and expenditures.

BACKGROUND

Concerns for Port Security

Government leaders and security experts are worried that the maritime transportation system could be used by terrorists to smuggle personnel, weapons of mass destruction, or other dangerous materials into the United States. They are also concerned that ships in U.S. ports, particularly large commercial cargo ships or cruise ships, could be attacked by terrorists. Experts are concerned that a large-scale terrorist attack at a U.S. port could not only cause local death and damage, but also paralyze global maritime commerce. The 9/11 Commission reported that, "While commercial aviation remains a possible target, terrorists may turn their attention to other modes. Opportunities to do harm are as great, or greater, in maritime and surface transportation. Initiatives to secure shipping containers have just begun."[3]

In response to concerns for port security, on November 14, 2002, Congress passed S. 1214, as amended, the Maritime Transportation Security Act of 2002 (MTSA), and the President signed it into law as P.L. 107-295 on November 25, 2002. The Coast Guard and Maritime Transportation Act of 2004 was signed into law as P.L. 108-293 on August 9, 2004. Title VIII of the act adds specificity to some of the provisions in MTSA. On December 17, 2004, the Intelligence Reform and Terrorism Prevention Act of 2004 (P.L. 108-458) was signed into law. This act implements the transportation security-related recommendations of the 9/11 Commission with respect to maritime transportation.

There is continuing debate about whether current efforts to improve port security are adequate in addressing the threat. While many agree that Coast Guard and CBP initiatives to address the threat are strengthening the security of the maritime transportation system, they contend that these initiatives represent only a framework for building a maritime security regime, and that significant gaps in security still remain.

Features of the U.S. Maritime System

U.S. Ports. The U.S. maritime system includes more than 300 sea and river ports with more than 3,700 cargo and passenger terminals and more than 1,000 harbor channels spread along thousands of miles of coastline.[4]

Transportation firms tend to concentrate traffic through major cargo hubs because of the high cost of their infrastructure.[5] The top 50 ports in the United States account for about 90% of all cargo tonnage and 25 U.S. ports account for 98% of all container shipments.[6] Energy products are concentrated at particular ports. For instance, almost one-quarter of California's imported crude oil is offloaded in one geographically confined area.[7]

Commercial Ships Using U.S. Ports. In 2003, approximately 6,000 commercial ships made approximately 60,000 U.S. port calls.[8] Most ships calling at U.S. ports are foreign owned and foreign crewed; less than 3% of U.S. overseas trade is carried on U.S.-flag vessels.[9]

Cargo Containers. Container ships are a growing segment of maritime commerce — and the focus of much of the attention on seaport security. Container ships carry stacks of marine containers loaded with a wide variety of goods. A large container ship can carry more than 3,000 containers, of which several hundred might be offloaded at a given port.

A marine container is similar to a truck trailer without wheels; standard sizes are 8 x 8 x 20 feet or 8 x 8 x 40 feet. Once offloaded from ships, they are transferred to rail cars or tractor-trailers or barges for inland transportation. Over-the-road weight regulations generally limit the cargo load of a 40 foot container to approximately 45,000 pounds. The estimated world inventory of containers is about 12 million. Container ships tend to carry higher-value cargo than other types of cargo ships. While they represent only 11% of annual tonnage, they account for 66% of the total value of U.S. maritime overseas trade. Containerized imports are dominated by consumer goods, such as clothing, shoes, electronics, and toys. U.S. automakers also import large quantities of parts in containers. Containerized exports are dominated by wastepaper, forest products, chemicals, and agricultural products.[10]

More than 9 million cargo containers enter U.S. sea ports each year. For comparison, over 13 million trucks and rail cars cross the Canadian and Mexican borders. CBP analyzes cargo manifest information for each container to decide which to target for closer inspection, based on such factors as origin, destination, shipper, and container contents. Only a small portion have their contents physically inspected by CBP. Physical inspection could include scanning the entire container with a sophisticated x-ray or gamma ray machine, unloading the contents of a container, or both.[11]

Importance of the U.S. Maritime System

Economic Importance. Ships are the primary mode of transportation for world trade. Ships carry approximately 80% of world trade by volume.[12] The United States is the world's leading maritime trading nation, accounting for nearly 20% (measured in tons) of the annual world ocean-borne overseas trade. Ships carry more than 95% of the nation's non-North American trade by weight and 75% by value. Trade now accounts for 25% of U.S. Gross Domestic Product (GDP), up from 11% in 1970. Over the next two decades, the total volume of domestic and international trade is expected to double.

Given the importance of maritime trade to the U.S. and world economies, disruptions to that trade can have immediate and significant economic impacts.[13] By one estimate, the cost to the U.S. economy of port closures on the West Coast due to a labor-management dispute was approximately $1 billion per day for the first five days, rising sharply thereafter.[14]

The container shipping system is designed for speed and efficiency. Transportation services are a critical component of the global, low-inventory (i.e., just-in-time) distribution model that many manufacturers have adopted. Most industries in the United States use some imported components from overseas suppliers. By bringing parts to a plant just before they are needed for assembly, manufacturers can save money on warehouse space and inventory carrying costs. Transport efficiencies permit warehouse requirements to be minimized. Lean inventories in turn have contributed to business productivity. From 1980 to 2000, according to one study, business logistics costs dropped from 16.1% of U.S. GDP to 10.1%.[15]

Given the dependence of the United States and the global economy on a highly efficient maritime transportation system, many experts acknowledge that slowing the flow of trade to inspect all inbound containers, or at least a statistically significant random selection would be "economically intolerable."[16] Supply chain analysts are concerned that increased security-related delay at seaports could threaten the efficiency gains achieved in inventory management over the past two decades by forcing companies to hold larger inventories.

Enhanced security has benefits as well as costs. Many experts see economic benefits to tighter control over maritime commerce. Resources put towards seaport security can also reduce cargo theft, narcotic and migrant smuggling, trade law violations, the accidental introduction of invasive species, and the cost of cargo insurance. Improved planning for responding to a terrorist attack at a seaport could also improve responses to other emergencies, such as natural disasters or transportation accidents. New technologies intended to convert the sea container into a "smart box," such as electronic seals, sensors, or tracking devices, could also improve shipment integrity, help carriers improve their equipment utilization, and help cargo owners track their shipments. In response to the terrorist threat, the CBP has accelerated development of its new information management system, the Automated Commercial Environment (ACE). This system will assist CBP in evaluating cargo manifest information for high risk shipments but will also speed the customs filing process for U.S. importers.[17]

National Security Importance. In addition to its economic significance, the marine transportation system is vital for national security. The Departments of Defense and Transportation have designated 17 U.S. seaports as strategic because they are necessary for use by DOD in the event of a major military deployment. Thirteen of these ports are commercial seaports. During Desert Storm, 90% of all military equipment and supplies were shipped from U.S. strategic ports. The deployment required over 312 vessels from 18 commercial and military ports in the United States. As the GAO has reported, "If the strategic ports (or the ships carrying military supplies) were attacked, not only could massive civilian casualties be sustained, but DOD could also lose precious cargo and time and be forced to rely heavily on its overburdened airlift capabilities."[18]

Port Security Threat Scenarios

Security experts are concerned about a variety of terrorist threat scenarios at U.S. ports. Among other things, they are concerned that terrorists could:

- use commercial cargo containers to smuggle terrorists, nuclear, chemical, or biological weapons, components thereof, or other dangerous materials into the United States;
- seize control of a large commercial cargo ship and use it as a collision weapon for destroying a bridge or refinery located on the waterfront;
- sink a large commercial cargo ship in a major shipping channel, thereby blocking all traffic to and from the port;
- attack a large ship carrying a volatile fuel (such as liquefied natural gas) and detonate the fuel so as to cause a massive in-port explosion;
- attack an oil tanker in a port or at an offshore discharge facility[19] so as to disrupt the world oil trade and cause large-scale environmental damage;
- seize control of a ferry (which can carry hundreds of passengers) or a cruise ship (which can carry more than 3,000 passengers, of whom about 90% are usually U.S. citizens) and threaten the deaths of the passengers if a demand is not met;
- attack U.S. Navy ships in an attempt to kill U.S. military personnel, damage or destroy a valuable U.S. military asset, and (in the case of nuclear-powered ships) cause a radiological release.
- use land around a port to stage attacks on bridges, refineries located on the waterfront, or other port facilities.

Some of these scenarios (or similar ones) have already come to pass elsewhere. For example, in October 2002, the French oil tanker *Limberg* appears to have been attacked by a bomb-laden boat off the coast of Yemen, killing one crewman aboard the tanker, damaging the ship, and causing an oil spill.[20] In October 2001, Italian authorities arrested on terrorism charges an Egyptian-born Canadian citizen found with high-tech equipment (including a satellite phone and a computer) and other personal possessions in a cargo container in an Italian port.[21] In October 2000, the U.S. Navy destroyer Cole was attacked by a bomb-laden boat during a refueling stop in the harbor of Aden, Yemen, killing 17 sailors, injuring 39 others, and causing damage to the ship that cost about $250 million to repair.[22] In 1985, terrorists seized the cruise ship *Achille Lauro* in the Mediterranean and held its passengers hostage, killing one of them.

Much concern has focused on the threat that a sea container could be used to smuggle a nuclear weapon into the United States. Experts are concerned that if a nuclear weapon in a container aboard a ship in port is detonated, it could not only kill tens of thousands of people and cause massive destruction, but could also paralyze the movement of cargo containers globally, thereby shutting down world trade.[23]

Port and Ship Vulnerabilities to Terrorist Attack

Port Facilities. Port areas and ships in ports have many vulnerabilities to potential terrorist attack. Port areas have very large landside perimeters to secure, giving terrorists many potential landside points of entry. Some ports are located immediately adjacent to built-up urban areas, giving terrorists places to hide while approaching or escaping from port areas. Large numbers of trucks move in and out of ports, making it possible for terrorists to use a truck to bring themselves and their weapons into a port. Many ports harbor fishing and recreational boats that terrorists could use to mask their approach to a target ship.

Ships. Commercial cargo ships at pier or at anchorage in harbor are stationary, and those moving through port do so at slow speeds, making them easy to intercept by a fast-moving boat. Commercial cargo ships are generally unarmed and have very small crews, making them vulnerable to seizure by a small group of armed people, as proven by modern-day pirates. In the 1990s, the number of reported attacks on cargo ships by pirates tripled.[24] Most pirate attacks occur while the ship is in port. Although most attacks occur in Southeast Asian waters on foreign-flag freighters, U.S. shippers are likely to be among the owners of cargo onboard. It can also be noted that some experts believe there is a link between piracy and terrorism — that the goal of some acts of piracy may be to raise money to finance terrorist operations. The *Financial Times* has reported an incident where a chemical tanker in the south Pacific was boarded by pirates who practiced steering the vessel at varying speeds for several hours.[25]

The lack of transparency in ship registration has been a longstanding concern. An Organization for Economic Cooperation and Development (OECD) study on the ownership and control of ships reports that:

> Not only does perfect transparency not exist, but in fact anonymity seems to be the rule rather than the exception, and not only is it permitted, but in many cases positively encouraged. This enables terrorists and would be terrorists to remain intimately involved in the operation of their vessels, while maintaining totally hidden, through the use of relatively simple mechanisms that are readily available and legally tolerated in almost all jurisdictions.[26]

Unscrupulous ship owners are known to mask their identity by re-registering their vessels under fictitious corporate names and renaming and repainting their ships. Shipowners can register their vessels in "flag of convenience" countries which may have lax regulations and require little information from the applicants. According to press reports, U.S. intelligence officials believe they have identified 15 cargo ships that have links to al Qaeda.[27]

Container Shipments. The complexity of the process for completing containerized shipments makes it more difficult to ensure the integrity of this type of cargo.[28] Unlike other cargo ships whose loading process occurs at the port and whose cargo is often owned by a single company, container ships carry cargo from hundreds of companies and the containers are loaded away from the port at individual company warehouses. A typical single container shipment may involve a multitude of parties and generate 30 to 40 documents. A single container could also carry cargo for several customers, thus multiplying the number of parties and documents involved. The parties involved in a shipment usually include the exporter, the importer, a freight forwarder, a customs broker, a customs inspector, inland transportation provider(s) (which may include more than one trucker or railroad), the port operators, possibly a feeder ship, and the ocean carrier. Each transfer of the container from one party to the next is a point of vulnerability in the supply chain. The security of each transfer facility and the trustworthiness of each company is therefore critical in the overall security of the shipment. It is also important to keep in mind that not all U.S.-bound containers arrive at U.S. ports. Half of the containers discharged at the Port of Montreal, for instance, move by truck or rail for cities in the northeastern or midwestern United States.[29] Also, many containers that enter U.S. waters are bound for other nations.

Maritime Crimes. Security experts warn that terrorists attempting to use a container to smuggle a weapon of mass destruction or components thereof into the United States could purchase a known exporter with a long and trustworthy shipping record. Drug smugglers have been known to employ this strategy to disguise their contraband in otherwise legitimate cargo. While both the Coast Guard and CBP are experienced in the marine environment with the "war on drugs," they recognize that terrorism is a different kind of threat. Among other things, drug smugglers are often interested in finding a smuggling method that can be used over and over to make multiple shipments. This permits the Coast Guard and CBP to look for certain patterns of operation among drug smugglers. Terrorists, on the other hand, are more likely to be interested in using a particular method of attack only once, to carry out a particular terrorist operation. This makes the tactic of looking for patterns of operation potentially much less useful. Another difference concerns the potential consequences of failure to detect and intercept. Given the tremendous amount of cargo arriving at seaports, the mission of interdicting illegal drugs or a weapon of mass destruction is often described as searching for the needle in the haystack. In the case of the weapon of mass destruction, however, the potential consequence of not finding the so-called needle is much greater.

The incidence of other shipping-related crimes also attests to the challenges faced in improving port security. The National Cargo Security Council estimates that cargo theft domestically ranges between $10 billion and $15 billion annually.[30] The FBI believes much of this theft occurs in or near seaports.[31] Identifying where cargo theft occurs in the transportation system may help identify where terrorist infiltration could occur.

Government Authorities at Seaports

Port Governance and Financing. In considering how to enhance seaport security, it is important to know how they are governed and operated. The governing structure of ports varies from place to place. While the federal government has jurisdiction over interstate and foreign commerce and designated federal waterway channels, state or local governments have ownership over ports. There are ports which are part of state government and others which are part of city government. The Port Authority of New York and New Jersey and the Delaware River Port Authority are examples of bi-state or regional port agencies.

Ports can be a subsidiary of a public agency but may be structured to act as a private sector corporation. Most ports are "landlord ports," which means the port provides the basic services and infrastructure but the tenant, such as a terminal operator, performs most of the activity. "Operating ports" both generate and carry out most of the activity at the port. In addition to city law enforcement personnel, some port authorities also have their own police forces.

Depending on how they are structured, ports finance infrastructure improvements through a variety of means. Some may levy taxes, if they are granted this authority. Ports may also pay for infrastructure with the general funds they receive from the governments they are a part of, from operating revenues, general obligation bonds, revenue bonds, trust fund monies, or loan guarantees. Most ports generally break even or are minimally profitable.[32]

Federal Agencies Involved in Port Security. Federal agencies involved in port security include the Coast Guard, the Bureau of Customs and Border Protection (CBP), and the Transportation Security Agency (TSA), all of which are housed in the Department of Homeland Security (DHS), and the Maritime Administration (MARAD). The Coast Guard and CBP are the two federal agencies with the strongest presence at seaports.

Coast Guard. The Coast Guard is the nation's principal maritime law enforcement authority and the lead federal agency for the maritime component of homeland security, including port security.[33] Among other things, the Coast Guard is responsible for evaluating, boarding, and inspecting commercial ships as they approach U.S. waters, for countering terrorist threats in U.S. ports, and for helping to protect U.S. Navy ships in U.S. ports. A high-ranking Coast Guard officer in each port area serves as the Captain of the Port (COTP), who is lead federal official responsible for the security and safety of the vessels and waterways in his or her geographic zone. Under the terms of the Ports and Waterways Safety Act of 1972 (P.L. 92-340) and the recently enacted Maritime Transportation Security Act of 2002, the Coast Guard has responsibility to protect vessels and harbors from subversive acts.

Bureau of Customs and Border Protection. The Bureau of Customs and Border Protection (CBP) is the federal agency with principal responsibility for inspecting cargoes, including cargo containers, that commercial ships bring into U.S. ports and for the examination and inspection of ship crews and cruise ship passengers for ships arriving in U.S. ports from any foreign port. Prior to the establishment of the CBP, customs and immigration functions at U.S. borders were conducted separately by the Department of the Treasury's U.S. Customs Service and the Department of Justice's Immigration and Naturalization Service.

Transportation Security Administration. TSA is an agency created by the Aviation and Transportation Security Act of 2001 (P.L. 107-71). Initially, its focus was the security of air transportation but it is responsible for the security of all modes of transportation, cargo and passenger.

Maritime Administration. MARAD, which is part of the Department of Transportation (DOT), is a civilian agency that supports the U.S. commercial maritime industry. MARAD publishes regular Maritime Security Reports and a national planning guide on port security. MTSA requires MARAD to publish a revised version of its national planning guide on port security.

Port Security Initiatives by Federal Agencies

Coast Guard. In response to the terrorist attacks of September 11, 2001, the Coast Guard created the largest port-security operation since World War II. Coast Guard cutters and aircraft were diverted from more distant operating areas to patrol U.S. ports and coastal waters. The Coast Guard began to maintain security zones around waterside facilities, Navy ships, and cruise and cargo ships entering or leaving port. Coast Guard port security teams began to inspect certain high-interest vessels, and Coast Guard sea marshals began escorting certain ships transiting the harbor.

To counter the terrorist threat, the Coast Guard and CBP have sought to improve the quality and advance the timing of information submitted to them by shippers and carriers so that they can better evaluate the terrorist risk of ships, cargo, or crew bound for the United States. By increasing their knowledge of the various parties in the marine environment it is hoped that federal authorities will be better able to separate the bad from the good without impeding the flow of legitimate commerce. In support of this goal, the Coast Guard has instituted new reporting requirements for ships entering and leaving U.S. harbors. The former 24-hour advance Notice of Arrival (NOA) has been extended to a 96-hour NOA. The NOA includes detailed information on the crew, passengers, cargo, and the vessel itself.

The Coast Guard has also developed the concept of maritime domain awareness (MDA). MDA involves fusing intelligence information with information from public, private, commercial, and international sources to provide a more complete picture of potential maritime security threats. The Coast Guard will use this picture to support a risk-management approach to preventing or mitigating terrorist threats through the use of actionable knowledge.[34] In support of the MDA effort, the Coast Guard is expanding a vessel tracking system (the Automatic Identification System) to monitor ship traffic in harbors and is underway on a multibillion dollar effort (the Deepwater program) to replace and modernize its aging vessels and aircraft.[35]

On October 22, 2003 the Coast Guard issued final rules implementing MTSA.[36] These regulations became effective on November 21, 2003.

Bureau of Customs and Border Protection. Among the programs CBP has initiated to counter the terrorist threat are the Container Security Initiative (CSI) and the Customs-Trade Partnership Against Terrorism (C-TPAT). CSI is a series of bilateral, reciprocal agreements that, among other things, allow CBP personnel at selected foreign ports to pre-screen U.S.-bound containers. In order to give inspectors the data and time they need to pre-screen containers, CBP issued a new rule requiring that information about an ocean shipment be transmitted to CBP 24 hours *before* the cargo is loaded at a foreign port onto a U.S.-bound vessel. Previously, ocean carriers did not submit this information until the ship arrived at a U.S. port. CBP is also requiring more comprehensive and specific cargo information so it can more efficiently evaluate individual container shipments for risks of terrorism. More detailed descriptions are intended to help speed up non-intrusive inspections of high risk containers by reducing the number of containers inspectors need to unload for closer examination. The rationale of CSI is that a nuclear weapon or a radiological "dirty bomb"[37] that enters a U.S. port could be detonated, before the ship is inspected.[38]

C-TPAT, initiated in April 2002, offers importers expedited processing of cargo if they comply with CBP guidelines for securing their entire supply chain. Businesses that sign up for the program are required, among other things, to conduct a comprehensive self-assessment of their supply chain and submit a completed questionnaire to CBP that describes their current security practices. If CBP certifies an applicant, they may benefit from a reduced number of cargo inspections, thus reducing the risk of shipment delay.

Transportation Security Administration. The Transportation Security Administration in conjunction with CBP is conducting the Operation Safe Commerce (OSC) pilot project.[39] The goal of OSC is to verify the contents of containers at their point of loading, ensure the physical integrity of containers in transit, and track their movement through each mode of transport from origin to final destination. Container tracking is a key area of debate on cargo security. Various "smart container" devices are being developed that would provide real-time location information and container tampering notification. The challenge is developing a device that can withstand the harsh ocean environment, be relatively inexpensive, and reliable enough not to trigger false alarms. TSA is also field-testing a Transportation Worker Identification Credential (TWIC) for workers in all modes of transportation that will be used to control access to secure areas of cargo and passenger facilities. The agency has developed a "Maritime Self-Assessment Risk Module" to assist port terminal and vessel owners in developing their security plans as required by MTSA.

Maritime Administration. MARAD, along with the Coast Guard, CBP, and TSA, is part of the Container Working Group which has made classified recommendations on how best to ensure the security of marine container transportation. MARAD has also developed a curriculum for training maritime security personnel.

International Institutions. In June 2002, the Group of Eight Nations identified the IMO and the World Customs Organization (WCO) as two institutions that should develop global initiatives to improve maritime security.

At its December 2002 conference, the IMO adopted a new chapter to the Safety of Life at Sea (SOLAS) Convention entitled International Ship and Port Facility Security (ISPS) Code.[40] The code contains both mandates and voluntary measures to improve maritime security. IMO member governments had until July 1, 2004 to implement the new regulations. The code largely parallels the requirements called for in MTSA.[41]

The World Customs Organization is a Brussels-based entity that has been working towards simplifying and harmonizing customs procedures to improve the efficiency of cross-border trade.[42] Currently, 164 countries accounting for 99% of world trade are members of the WCO. In June 2002, the WCO created a task force to draft a "Resolution on Security and Facilitation of the International Supply Chain" which they completed in June 2003. In May 2005, the WCO issued its Framework of Standards to Secure and Facilitate Global Trade. The framework sets out principles for advance, electronic reporting of cargo and shipper data and requires importers to verify security measures taken by its suppliers.

Recent Law on Port Security

The bill creating the new Department of Homeland Security (DHS), was passed by the Senate on November 19, 2002 and by the House on November 22, 2002, and signed into law as P.L. 107-296 on November 25, 2002. The DHS incorporates the Coast Guard, the former Customs Service, and TSA, among others.[43]

The Maritime Transportation Security Act of 2002 was passed by Congress on November 14, 2002 and signed into law as P.L. 107-295 on November 25, 2002. The act creates a U.S. maritime security system and requires federal agencies, ports, and vessel owners to take numerous steps to upgrade security. The act requires the Coast Guard to develop national and regional area maritime transportation security plans. It requires ports, waterfront terminals, and certain types of vessels to develop security and incident response plans with approval from the Coast Guard. The act authorizes CBP to require that cargo manifest information for inbound or outbound shipments be provided to the agency electronically prior to the arrival or departure of the cargo. This information may be shared with other appropriate federal agencies. The legislation calls on the Department of Transportation to determine the level of funding needed for a grant program that will finance security upgrades. The act also authorizes $90 million in grants for research and development in improving cargo inspection, detecting nuclear materials, and improving the physical security of marine containers. A dispute over how to pay for the cost of enhancing port security was resolved by eliminating controversial user fee provisions from the conference report (funding issues are discussed further below).

The Trade Act of 2002 (P.L. 107-210) was enacted into law on August 6, 2002. Section 343 provides authority to CBP to issue regulations requiring the electronic transmission of cargo information to CBP prior to the shipments' exportation or importation into the United States.

The Coast Guard and Maritime Transportation Act of 2004 was signed into law as P.L. 108-293 on August 9, 2004. Title VIII of the act contains a number of provisions related to maritime security, many of which add specificity to provisions in MTSA. Among other things, the act requires the DHS to submit a plan to Congress implementing a maritime intelligence system (section 803); it requires the DHS to submit a plan for a maritime security grant program, including recommendations on how funds should be allocated (section 804); it requires the Coast Guard to report on the implementation and use of joint operational centers at certain U.S. ports (section 807); it requires the DOT to investigate and examine sensors that are able to track marine containers throughout their supply chain and detect hazardous and radioactive materials within the containers (section 808); it requires the DHS to report on the costs of vessel and container inspections, and a plan for implementing secure systems of transportation, including the need for and feasibility to inspect and monitor intermodal shipping containers within the United States (section 809).

The week of December 6, 2004, Congress passed the Intelligence Reform and Terrorism Prevention Act of 2004 (P.L. 108-458). The act imposes an urgency on DHS's efforts in strengthening maritime security by imposing deadlines on the agency in planning and carrying out certain maritime security activities that were called for in MTSA. This includes a deadline of April 1, 2005 for completion of a national maritime security plan; a deadline of December 31, 2004 for completion of facility and vessel vulnerability assessments; and deadlines for a deployment plan for TWIC, a status report on standards for seafarer identification, and a status report on establishing performance standards for container seals and locks. The act also requires DHS to create a terrorism "watch list" for passengers and crew aboard cruise ships.

ISSUES FOR CONGRESS

The challenge of port security raises several potential issues for Congress. Some Members of Congress, who have introduced their own versions of maritime security legislation, are concerned that MTSA does not go far enough in its requirements. In addition to considering further port security legislation, Congress is debating whether the federal government is providing enough funds to port authorities and border agencies for improving port security. Congress is also considering how to pay for port security.

Addressing the Threat

A major concern for Congress is assessing whether the Nation is addressing the threat to maritime security with enough urgency. Despite the progress that has been made in strengthening port security thus far, many security officials still describe seaports as "wide open" and "very vulnerable" to terrorist attack.[44] Seaports, along with air cargo, general aviation, and mass transit were identified in a recent GAO report as the "major vulnerabilities" remaining in the nation's transportation system.[45] The GAO found that "an effective port security environment may be many years away." While many agree that CSI, C-TPAT, OSC, and MDA, are sound strategies for addressing the threat, they contend that these programs represent only a framework for building a maritime security regime, and that significant gaps in security still remain. In the words of one security expert,[46]

> Right now, none of these initiatives has changed the intermodal transportation environment sufficiently to fundamentally reduce the vulnerability of the cargo container as a means of terrorism. However, all are important stepping-off points for building an effective risk management approach to container security — a foundation that simply did not exist prior to September 11, 2001.

In its oversight role, Congress is examining the effectiveness of these programs in addressing the terrorist threat, whether they are proceeding at sufficient pace, and whether enough resources are being provided to implement these and other security initiatives.

Some observers and Members of Congress are concerned that initiatives to fill gaps in port security are not proceeding at a sufficient pace. TSA's program to credential all transportation workers and its effort to develop a "smart-box" to ensure the integrity of container shipments has also been criticized for moving forward too slowly. Some argue that the security funding provided to seaports, especially when compared to the amount provided to airports, is woefully inadequate.

Others argue that current efforts to improve port security are proceeding at an unprecedented pace. They note that the IMO, with leadership from the U.S. Coast Guard, agreed to new international port security measures within a year. They also note that the Coast Guard issued final rules implementing MTSA within a year after becoming law. During Operation Liberty Shield, (March 17, 2003 through April 16, 2003) the Coast Guard and CBP demonstrated their ability to rapidly intensify port security operations by increasing ship and cargo inspections, increasing air and surface patrols, escorting more ships through harbors, and other activities.[47]

Funding Port Security

According to many, the unresolved debate over how to pay for port security is stalling efforts to improve port security. The debate is over whether port security should be paid for with federal revenues, by state and local governments, by the maritime industry, or by a cost sharing arrangement among all of the above. The Coast Guard roughly estimates the cost of implementing the new IMO security code and the security provisions in MTSA to be approximately $1.5 billion for the first year and $7.3 billion over the succeeding decade.[48] Congress has provided over $650 million through FY2005 in direct federal grants to ports to improve their physical and operational security. This is in addition to the budgets of the Coast Guard, Bureau of Customs and Border Protection, TSA, and other federal agencies involved in port security.[49] Advocates for more spending argue that the federal funds provided to port authorities thus far are woefully inadequate, particularly when compared to airports. Skeptics of additional spending argue that taxpayers should not provide funds to large and profitable corporations to secure infrastructure that is in their own financial interest to do so.

Sources of Funds. A dispute over how to finance security requirements arose during the conference committee on MTSA. Senator Hollings proposed creating a system of user fees on ship cargo as a means of generating funds for port security upgrades required in the legislation. Other conferees opposed this proposal, calling the user fees a tax. Some policymakers contend that without providing a funding source, the act amounts to an unfunded mandate.

Port authorities, ocean carriers, and shippers argue that port security is a national concern and therefore the federal government should finance it through general revenues. Others argue that the maritime industry should finance port security through user fees because it is a direct beneficiary of improved security as it reduces cargo theft and other economic damages.[50]

Proponents of user fees contend that user surcharges are an effective means of ensuring improved security because they would provide a more secure and predictable source of funding than annual appropriations. They propose that a port security trust fund be created in a manner that prevents the user fees from being spent on anything other than port security. If such a port security trust fund were created, they argue, port security would not have to compete with other funding priorities in the annual appropriations process. Some economists contend that a user fee system is also more efficient than direct subsidies because the users of the service being provided (in this case port security) are likely to demand that policymakers spend the funds in the most productive manner.

Allocating Resources. An issue of likely interest to Congress is how to allocate resources appropriately to the various ports. Maximum security is prohibitively expensive. Therefore, it is important to properly identify specific security areas that have the greatest vulnerability and apportion funds accordingly. Criteria could include a port's relative economic importance and its proximity to an urban or sensitive area. The 9/11 Commission criticized the TSA for lacking a strategic plan for systematically analyzing transportation assets, risks, costs, and benefits in order to allocate limited resources in the most cost-effective way.[51] The Inspector General of the DHS was critical of port security grant award decisions made thus far and made recommendations for improving them.[52]

Resources for Foreign Ports. In addition to funding security at U.S. ports, there is also the issue of finding resources for improving security at foreign ports, especially in developing countries that may not be able to afford the technology to improve their ports' security. The IMO's recent adoption of new security measures includes a statement inviting the Secretary General of the IMO to give early consideration to establishing a "Maritime Security Trust Fund" for the purpose of providing financial support in developing countries for strengthening their maritime security infrastructure.[53]

Balancing Security and Commerce

Security experts argue that perfect maritime security can only be achieved by shutting down the transportation system. As one observer stated, "a harbor without ships is safe, but that is not what harbors are built for."[54] The issue for Congress is how to increase port security to desired levels while minimizing the economic impacts associated with impeding the maritime trade system. When security experts speak of significant gaps still remaining in maritime security, they are often referring to the credibility problems associated with the container loading and screening process overseas and the true identity of ships and their crew on the high seas.

Point of Origin Cargo Security. A major area of concern is ensuring the integrity of cargo as it begins its transit to the United States from its overseas origin. Point of origin security is necessary because inspecting cargo on the high seas is practically impossible and inspecting cargo upon its arrival at a U.S. port could be too late to prevent a terrorist event. Ensuring that the container was not stuffed with illegitimate cargo at the overseas factory, that the loaded container was not tampered with while trucked to the port of loading, and ensuring that the cargo information reported to CBP is not fraudulent are all critical challenges in supply chain security. Congress is examining the effectiveness of C-TPAT, CSI, and OSC in ensuring the integrity of U.S. bound cargo at its overseas point of origin. Issues include what type of procedures are necessary to verify the legitimacy of cargo loaded into a container, what type of "smart box" devices should be required to ensure the physical integrity of the container while en route, and what specific information should cargo manifests contain to enable CBP to target shipments for closer inspection.

The GAO investigated how the CSI and C-TPAT programs were being implemented and found several shortcomings that need correction.[55] The GAO found that C-TPAT participants were benefitting from reduced scrutiny of their imported cargo after they had been certified into the program but before CBP had validated that the participants were indeed carrying out the promised security measures. The GAO also found that not all containers that CBP had targeted for inspection at the overseas loading port were being inspected by the host customs administration. The GAO found other flaws in these two programs and CBP has taken corrective action to address some of these flaws.[56]

Vessels Under Foreign Ownership and Control. There is no single sovereign power that regulates international shipping. MTSA requires the Coast Guard to report on foreign-flag vessels calling at U.S. ports, specifically those vessels with murky ownership histories, and to report on actions taken to improve the transparency of vessel registration procedures (section 112). In December 2002, as mentioned above, the

IMO adopted more stringent international standards for the security of vessels and ports.

Congress is likely to examine the effectiveness of Coast Guard and international efforts at raising the security level of ship operators. Skeptics contend that the new IMO regulations mostly offer the illusion of increased security. They contend that "flag of convenience" countries lack the resolve to enforce these standards and that the compliance documentation is too easy to manipulate in order to appear as legitimate operators.[57] While the United States enforces its standards when the Coast Guard selects arriving ships for boarding, their burden is greater if there is no effective international shipping regime that pre-screens substandard shipping.

International Considerations

In the wake of the terrorist attacks of September 11, 2001, a consensus emerged among experts involved in the issue that an effective solution for securing maritime trade requires creating an international maritime security regime. This regime would rely not on a single solution, such as increasing the number of container inspections, but rather on a layered approach with multiple lines of defense from the beginning to the final destination of a shipment. The first security perimeter in this "defense in depth" strategy would be at the overseas point of origin.[58] Security experts argue that an effective solution must start with preventing undesired items from entering the maritime transportation network, because if some of these items — particularly nuclear weapons or dirty bombs — reach a U.S. seaport, they could be detonated before inspectors could find them.

A related issue is whether raising international port security standards should become part of international trade agreements. Thus far, the United States' strategy has been to raise standards by working within the maritime transportation industry, such as through the IMO. However, some assert that given the strong link between maritime security and international trade, the United States could also pursue international port security standards as part of international trade agreements.

Standard vs. Site-Specific Measures

An additional issue for Congress is determining what elements of port security might be best addressed through across-the-board requirements that establish common standards and practices to be applied at all seaports, versus those elements of port security that might be best addressed through a tailored, bottom-up approach that employs measures that are designed to fit the specific circumstances and meet specific needs of each seaport.

Some observers, while acknowledging the need for site-specific measures, argue that a certain amount of uniform measures are necessary to help ensure that no seaport remains excessively vulnerable to terrorist attack. Other observers argue that while standardized measures make sense up to a point, the effort to implement such measures must not come at the expense of efforts to devise and implement site-specific security measures that respond to the unique characteristics of each port. Compared to commercial airports, seaports are generally more diverse in terms of their physical infrastructure and operations. As a result of this diversity in characteristics, each ship and port facility presents different risks and vulnerabilities.

Port authorities are also very concerned with finding the right balance between standard and port specific security regulations. Ports seek a level of uniformity in security requirements because they are concerned that their customers will move their business to competing ports where their goods may be cleared more quickly. At the same time, ports do not want to be held to inflexible federal standards. They are concerned that setting security benchmarks may waste time and resources if those benchmarks are not applicable at their port given their particular commodity mix or other unique circumstances.

Security Cards. In addition to improving the security infrastructure of U.S. ports, there is also the issue of ensuring the trustworthiness of the people who work in them. Issuing credentials for port workers illustrates the challenge of implementing standard security measures. One of the difficult questions is what should disqualify someone from holding a job in a port area. MTSA (Section 70105) requires the Secretary of Homeland Security to develop a transportation security card for port workers that would be used to limit access to secure areas in a port.[59] Among the items that would disqualify a port worker from obtaining a card would be a felony conviction within the last seven years that the Secretary believes could cause the individual to be a terrorism risk.[60] The USA PATRIOT Act (P.L. 107-273) passed in October 2001, requires background checks for truckers carrying hazardous materials. The TSA is developing a "Transportation Worker Identification Credential" (TWIC) Program that will use biometric cards issued to all transportation workers to limit access to secure areas in the nationwide transportation network.

Issuing transportation ID cards is an example of an across-the-board requirement. However, the difficulty of implementing such measures at specific ports is illustrated below:[61]

> ...Tampa offers a good example. Some of the port's major employers consist of ship repair companies that hire hundreds of workers for short-term projects as the need arises. Historically, according to port authority officials, these workers have included persons with criminal records. However, new state requirements for background checks, as part of issuing credentials, could deny such persons needed access to restricted areas of the port. From a security standpoint, excluding such persons may be advisable; but from an economic standpoint, a company may have difficulty filling jobs if it cannot include such persons in the labor pool.

Roles and Responsibilities

A major concern for U.S. policymakers is assigning roles and responsibilities for maritime security among federal agencies, among federal, state, and local agencies, and between government agencies and private industry. Clear roles and responsibilities are needed to prevent overlap, duplication of effort, and conflicting regulations. It is critical that the maritime trade community perceives that federal agencies are working in concert, otherwise the DHS's goal of a close partnership with industry in fighting terrorism may be frustrated.

Intelligence Sharing. The difficulty of detecting terrorist activity once it has entered the maritime system may point to the value of intelligence. Most acknowledge that there is just too much cargo, coming from all corners of the globe, to scrutinize each shipment thoroughly. Uncovering terrorist activity is likely to require "actionable" or precise intelligence identifying exactly which shipment to intercept. The GAO reports that "in surface transportation, timely information-sharing has been hampered by the lack of standard protocols to exchange information among federal, state, and local government agencies and private entities."[62] One barrier to more effective intelligence sharing with local port authorities may be that state and local government officials do not have the required security clearances.

Private Industry's Role. A broad policy question for Congress is how much of a role the private sector should have in enhancing maritime security. Many observers believe that businesses will worry more about near term profits than the remote possibility that their property will be attacked.[63] At the same time, most experts acknowledge that there are just too many cargo movements for the government to monitor on its own. Security experts believe that tightening control over maritime commerce requires that security be "embedded" into everyday business processes. CBP's C-TPAT program is intended to enlist the effort of the many companies involved in international container shipments. In its oversight responsibilities, Congress may evaluate the effectiveness of this program, particularly in ensuring the due diligence of maritime traders over the long term. Congress may consider how best to ensure sustained follow through on the part of C-TPAT participants. A "trust but verify" approach utilizing regular CBP security audits may be one strategy policymakers consider.

SELECTED PORT SECURITY LEGISLATION INTRODUCED IN THE 109TH CONGRESS

Several proposals have been introduced in the 109th Congress to improve port security. In the House, H.R. 163, introduced by Representative Millender-McDonald, would create a pilot program for the sealing of empty containers. H.R. 173, introduced by Representative Millender-McDonald, would amend the criminal code to include certain terrorist related acts in the marine environment as unlawful, require the Attorney General to coordinate port-related crime data collection, as well as other port security related provisions. H.R. 478, introduced by Representative Millender-McDonald, authorizes federal port security grants and the issuance of letters of intent to fund port security projects. H.R. 785, introduced by Representative Stearns, would create a federal database for the collection of cargo crime data. H.R. 1731, introduced by Representative Harman, authorizes federal port security grants to be funded from Customs import duties. H.R. 1817, the DHS Authorization Act for FY2006, which passed the House on May 18, 2005, contains numerous provisions related to port security.

In the Senate, S. 3, introduced by Senator Gregg, makes unlawful certain acts related to maritime security. S. 12, introduced by Senator Biden, would accelerate the deployment of radiation detection portal equipment at U.S. and foreign seaports and establish a tanker security initiative, among other provisions. S. 376, introduced by Senator Hutchinson, requires the DHS to develop a strategy to ensure the security of intermodal shipping containers, whether imported, exported, or shipped domestically and requires that no less than half of all imported containers be equipped with "smart box" technology by 2007. S. 378, introduced by Senator Biden, and reported by the Committee on the Judiciary on April 21, 2005, increases penalties for certain maritime crimes. S. 744, introduced by Senator Nelson, requires the Maritime Administration to create a Caribbean Basin Port Security Assistance Program. S. 855, introduced by Senator Collins, parallels H.R. 1731. S. 1052, introduced by Senator Stevens, would establish additional joint harbor operational centers for port security, establish a deadline of January 1, 2006 for the issuance of the TWIC card, require importers to submit additional manifest data as part of the 24 hour rule, increase the number of CSI inspectors, establish and develop a plan for the random inspection of shipping containers, require DHS to conduct a study on the desirability of creating a user fee for funding port security, as well as other provisions related to port security.

REFERENCES

[1] This report was prepared with assistance from Jennifer Lake, Jonathan Medalia, and Ronald O'Rourke.
[2] For other CRS products on the subject of maritime security, see CRS Report RS21293, *Terrorist Nuclear Attacks on Seaports: Threat and Response*; CRS Report RS21125, *Homeland Security:*

	Coast Guard Operations — Background and Issues for Congress; CRS Report RS21230, *Homeland Security: Navy Operations — Background and Issues for Congress*; CRS Report RS21997, *Port and Maritime Security: Potential for Terrorist Nuclear Attack Using Oil Tankers.*
[3]	*The 9/11 Commission Report: Final Report of the National Commission on Terrorist Attacks Upon the United States,* New York: W.W. Norton, 2004, p. 391.
[4]	For further information on the U.S. maritime system, see U.S. DOT, Maritime Admin., *An Assessment of the U.S. Marine Transportation System,* Sept. 1999. Available at [http://www.marad.dot.gov/].
[5]	The U.S. Army Corps of Engineers' Navigation Data Center ranks U.S. ports by dollar value and tons of cargo imported and exported. See [http://www.iwr.usace.army.mil/ndc/].
[6]	U.S. Congress, House of Representatives, Maritime Transportation Security Act of 2002, Conference Report, H.Rept. 107-777, p. 4.
[7]	*How Did This Happen?* ed. James F. Hoge, Jr. and Gideon Rose (New York: Public Affairs, 2001), p.186.
[8]	U.S. Maritime Administration, *Vessel Calls at U.S. Ports, 2003,* July 2004.
[9]	The Maritime Component," *Sea Power,* August 2001.
[10]	For a list of the top importers and exporters of containerized marine cargo, see "Inside the Box," *Journal of Commerce,* Aug. 12-18, 2002, p. 20A.
[11]	For further information on CBP's container inspection process, see CBP Fact Sheet: *The 5 Percent Myth vs. U.S. Customs and Border Protection Reality,* October 7, 2004.
[12]	United Nations Conference on Trade and Development (UNCTAD), *Review of Maritime Transport 2002.*
[13]	For further information, see OECD, *Security in Maritime Transport: Risk Factors and Economic Impact,* Maritime Transport Committee, July 2003.
[14]	Report of an Independent Task Force Sponsored by the Council on Foreign Relations, *America Still Unprepared — America Still in Danger,* October 2002, p. 23.

[15] Michael Wolfe, North River Consulting Group, *Freight Transportation Security and Productivity,* report prepared for U.S. DOT, EU/US Forum on Intermodal Freight Transport, Apr. 11-13, 2001.

[16] Admiral James M. Loy and Captain Robert G. Ross, "Global Trade, America's Achilles Heel," *Defense Horizons,* Feb. 2002.

[17] For further information on ACE, see [http://www.cbp.gov/xp/cgov/toolbox/about/ modernization/] (viewed 12/4/03).

[18] GAO, *Combating Terrorism, Actions Needed to Improve Force Protection for DOD Deployments through Domestic Seaports,* GAO-03-15, Oct. 2002.

[19] In an offshore "lightering" zone, a very large crude carrier (VLCC) or "supertanker" transfers part of its cargo to a smaller shuttle tanker that delivers the crude oil to the tank farm or refinery onshore. There are also offshore oil ports where a tanker discharges its cargo through a submerged pipeline that carries the cargo along the seabed to the onshore terminal.

[20] "Ships as Terrorist Targets," *American Shipper,* Nov. 2002, p.59.

[21] His lawyers argued that he was a Maronite Christian fleeing religious discrimination and personal legal problems in Egypt who was shipping his possessions to Canada and planned to fly from Rome to Montreal. (He was also carrying a plane ticket.) Charges against him were dropped and he was ordered freed from jail in mid-November 2001. (Italian Court Frees Canadian Suspect. *Toronto Star*, November 16, 2002.)

[22] CRS Report RS20721, *Terrorist Attack on U.S.S. Cole: Background and Issues for Congress.*

[23] U.S. Department of the Treasury, Customs Service. Robert Bonner, U.S. Customs Commissioner, Speech Before the Center for Strategic and International Studies, Washington, D.C., January 17, 2002. [http://www.cbp.gov/xp/cgov/newsroom/commissioner/speeches_statements/archives/jan172002.xml].

[24] U.S. DOT, *Surface Transportation Security: Vulnerabilities and Developing Solutions,* n.d., n.p.

[25] "The Maritime Threat from Al Qaeda," *Financial Times,* October 20, 2003.

[26] OECD, *Ownership and Control of Ships,* Maritime Transport Committee, March 2003, p. 5.

[27] See "15 Freighters Believed to Be Linked to al Qaeda," *Washington Post,* Dec. 31, 2002, p. A1. Also, "Terrorism - Bin Laden Group Shipping Interests Probed," *Lloyd's List,* Sept. 28, 2001.
[28] See, Arun Chatterjee, *An Overview of Security Issues Involving Marine Containers and Ports,* proceedings of the 2003 Transportation Research Board Annual Meeting, available on CD-ROM.
[29] Hoge and Rose, ed. *How Did This Happen?* p. 188.
[30] "Executive Viewpoint, Joe M. Baker, Jr. Exec. Director, NCSC," *Journal of Commerce,* May 8, 2002.
[31] "Cargo Crime Bill Hit," *Traffic World,* Oct. 9, 2000.
[32] U.S. DOT, Maritime Administration, *Public Port Finance Survey for FY1999,* Jan. 2001.
[33] The Navy and the Coast Guard agree that the Coast Guard is the lead federal agency for the maritime component of homeland security, and that the Navy's role is to support the Coast Guard in areas where the Coast Guard's capabilities are limited or lacking, such as air defense or antisubmarine warfare. For more on the Navy's role in homeland security, see CRS Report RS21230, *Homeland Security: Navy Operations — Background and Issues for Congress*, by Ronald O'Rourke.
[34] For further information on the Coast Guard as it relates to homeland security, see CRS Report RS21125, *Homeland Security: Coast Guard Operations — Background and Issues for Congress* by Ronald O'Rourke.
[35] For further information on the Deepwater program, see CRS Report RS21019, *Coast Guard Deepwater Program: Background and Issues for Congress* by Ronald O'Rourke.
[36] See 68 Federal Register 60447 (Oct. 22, 2003).
[37] A dirty bomb is a conventional explosive device with radioactive material wrapped around it. Detonating the device disperses the radioactive material, contaminating the area with radioactivity that can be difficult to clean. Dirty bombs are also known as radiological dispersion devices. For further information, see CRS Report RS21528, *Terrorist 'Dirty Bombs': A Brief Primer.*
[38] See also, GAO, *Summary of Challenges Faced in Targeting Oceangoing Cargo Containers for Inspection,* GAO-04-557T,

March 31, 2004. 67 Federal Register 70110-70112 (Nov. 2, 2002).
[39] For further information about the code, see [http://www.imo.org/home.asp].
[40] For further information on meeting this deadline, see GAO, *Maritime Security: Substantial Work Remains to Translate New Planning Requirements into Effective Port Security,* GAO-04-838, June 2004.
[41] For further information about the WCO and trade security, see [http://www.wcoomd.org/ie/ En/en.html].
[42] For further information, see CRS Report RL31549, *Department of Homeland Security: Consolidation of Border and Transportation Security Agencies,* by William J. Krouse.
[43] "Safe Harbors?" *Wall Street Journal,* April 21, 2003, p.B1.
[44] GAO, *Transportation Security, Post September 11th Initiatives and Long-Term Challenges,* April 1, 2003, GAO-03-616T.
[45] Stephen Flynn, "On The Record," *Government Executive Magazine,* October 1, 2003.
[46] For further information on Operation Liberty Shield, see CRS Report RS21475, *Operation Liberty Shield: Border, Transportation, and Domestic Security.*
[47] See 68 Federal Register 60464 (Oct. 22, 2002).
[48] See CRS Report RL32863, *Homeland Security Department: FY2006 Appropriations.*
[49] Representative Dana Rohrabacher introduced an amendment to H.R. 2557 that would allow ports to impose a per-container fee to pay for port security. Unlike Senator Hollings's user fee proposal, the fund would be administered locally by individual ports.
[50] *The 9/11 Commission Report: Final Report of the National Commission on Terrorist Attacks Upon the United States* (New York: W.W. Norton, 2004), p. 391.
[51] DHS, Office of Inspector General, *Review of the Port Security Grant Program,* OIG-05-10, January 2005.
[52] For further information, see [http://www.imo.org/home.asp].
[53] "Port Shutdown for Terrorist Incidents Could Cost Billions, Drill Shows," *CQ Homeland Security,* Dec. 5, 2002.

[54] GAO, *Homeland Security: Key Cargo Security Programs Can Be Improved,* GAO-05-466T, May 26, 2005.
[55] See Senate Committee on Homeland Security and Government Affairs, Subcommittee on Investigations, Hearing on CSI and C-TPAT, May 26, 2005.
[56] See, for example, William Langewiesche, "Anarchy at Sea," *Atlantic Monthly,* Sept. 2003, p. 50.
[57] A leading advocate for point of origin security is Stephen Flynn; see "Beyond Border Control," *Foreign Affairs,* Nov./Dec. 2000.
[58] For a status report on progress towards development of this card, see GAO Report GAO-05-106, *Port Security[:] Better Planning Needed to Develop and Operate Maritime Worker Identification Card Program,* December 2004.
[59] Preexisting regulations regarding the issuing of Coast Guard port security cards are contained at 33 C.F.R. Part 125 — Identification Credentials for Persons Requiring Access to Waterfront Facilities or Vessels.
[60] GAO, *Port Security, Nation Faces Formidable Challenges in Making New Initiatives Successful,* GAO-02-993T, p. 13.
[61] GAO, *Transportation Security, Post-September 11th Initiatives and Long-Term Challenges,* April 1, 2003, GAO-03-616T. The GAO also examined this issue in the maritime context, see GAO, *Maritime Security: New Structures Have Improved Information Sharing, but Security Clearance Processing Requires Further Attention,* April 2005, GAO-05-394.
[62] "Gaps in Our Defenses," *Baltimore Sun,* Feb. 12, 2003.

In: Port and Maritime Security
Editor: Jonathon P. Vesky

ISBN 1-59454-726-2
© 2008 Nova Science Publishers, Inc.

Chapter 3

MARITIME SECURITY: OVERVIEW OF ISSUES[*]

John F. Frittelli

ABSTRACT

In the wake of the terrorist attacks of September 11, 2001, port security has emerged as a significant part of the overall debate on U.S. homeland security. Many security experts believe ports are vulnerable to terrorist attack because of their size, easy accessibility by water and land, and the tremendous amount of cargo they handle. To raise port security standards, Congress passed the Maritime Transportation Security Act of 2002 (P.L. 107-295) in November 2002. In the 108th Congress, there is growing debate about whether current efforts to improve port securityare proceeding at sufficient pace and whether the nation is devoting enough resources for this purpose.

---

[*] From CRS Report RS21079; December 5, 2003.

CONCERNS FOR PORT SECURITY

Government leaders and security experts worry that the maritime transportation system could be used by terrorists to smuggle personnel, weapons of mass destruction, or other dangerous materials into the United States.[1] They are also concerned that ships in U.S. ports, particularly large commercial cargo ships or cruise ships, could be attacked by terrorists. A large-scale terrorist attack at a U.S. port, experts warn, could not only cause local death and damage, but also paralyze global maritime commerce.

Even before the terrorist attacks of September 11, 2001, government officials and security experts were concerned about the security of U.S. ports. In the fall of 2000, the Interagency Commission on Crime and Security in U.S. Seaports noted the vulnerability of U.S. seaports to terrorism. The report noted that while the FBI then considered the threat of terrorist attacks on U.S. seaports to be low, their vulnerability to such attacks was high.[2] To address the concerns raised in the report, Senator Hollings introduced S. 1214, the Maritime Transportation Security Act of 2001 on July 20, 2001. On November 14, 2002, Congress passed S. 1214, as amended, the Maritime Transportation Security Act of 2002 (MTSA), and the President signed it into law as P.L. 107-295 on November 25, 2002.

Features of the U.S. Maritime System

The U.S. maritime system includes more than 300 sea and river ports with more than 3,700 cargo and passenger terminals and more than 1,000 harbor channels spread along thousands of miles of coastline.[3] Transportation firms tend to concentrate traffic through major cargo hubs because of the high cost of their infrastructure.[4] The top 50 ports in the United States account for about 90% of all cargo tonnage and 25 U.S. ports account for 98% of all container shipments.[5]

In 2001, approximately 5,400 commercial ships made more than 60,000 U.S. port calls. Most ships calling U.S. ports are foreign owned and foreign crewed; less than 3% of U.S. overseas trade is carried on U.S.-flag vessels.[6] The lack of transparency in ship ownership has been a longstanding concern. Shipowners can register their ships in "flag of convenience" countries which may have lax regulations and require little information from the applicants.[7]

Container ships are a growing segment of maritime commerce – and the focus of much of the attention on seaport security. While they carry only 11% of annual tonnage, they account for 66% of the total value of U.S. maritime overseas trade. A large container ship can carry more than 3,000 containers, of which several hundred might be offloaded at a given port. A marine container is similar to a truck trailer without wheels; standard sizes are 8x8x20 feet or 8x8x40 feet. More than 6 million cargo containers from all corners of the globe enter U.S. seaports each year. The Bureau of Customs and Border Protection (CBP) analyzes cargo manifest information for each container to decide which to target for closer inspection but only a small percentage have their contents physically inspected by CBP.

Ships are the primary mode of transportation for world trade. Ships carry more than 95% of the nation's non-North American trade by weight and 75% by value. Waterborne cargo contributes about 7.5% to the U.S. gross domestic product.[8] Given the importance of maritime trade to the U.S. economy, disruptions to that trade can have immediate and significant economic impacts.

Recent Port Security Initiatives by Federal Authorities

Leading federal agencies involved in port security include the Coast Guard, the Bureau of Customs and Border Protection (CBP), and the Transportation Security Administration (TSA), all of which are housed in the Department of Homeland Security (DHS). To counter the terrorist threat, the Coast Guard and CBP have sought to improve the quality and advance the timing of information submitted to them by shippers and carriers so that they can better evaluate the terrorist risk of ships, cargo, passengers or crew destined for the United States. By increasing their knowledge of the various parties in the marine environment, it is hoped that federal inspectors will be better able to separate the bad from the good without impeding the flow of legitimate travel and commerce.

Coast Guard. The Coast Guard is the nation's principal maritime law enforcement authority and the lead federal agency for the maritime component of homeland security, including port security.[9] Among other things, the Coast Guard is responsible for evaluating, boarding, and inspecting commercial ships as they approach U.S. waters, for countering terrorist threats in U.S. ports, and for helping to protect U.S. Navy ships in U.S. ports. A high-ranking Coast Guard officer in each port area serves as the Captain of the Port (COTP), who is the lead federal official responsible for the security and safety of the vessels and waterways in his or her geographic zone. Under the terms of the Ports and Waterways Safety Act of 1972 (P.L. 92-340) and the recently enacted Maritime Transportation Security Act of 2002, the Coast Guard has responsibility to protect vessels and harbors from subversive acts. The Coast Guard issued final rules implementing MTSA on October 22, 2003 (see 68 Fed. Reg. 60448).

The Coast Guard refers to its efforts at improving its knowledge of the ships calling at U.S. ports as "Maritime Domain Awareness" (MDA). The Coast Guard has instituted new reporting requirements for ships entering U.S. harbors. The former 24-hour advance Notice of Arrival (NOA) has been extended to a 96-hour NOA. The NOA includes detailed information on the crew, passengers, cargo, and the vessel itself. The NOA is evaluated to select certain high-interest vessels for boarding by Coast Guard port security teams. Coast Guard sea marshals may also escort certain ships transiting the harbor.

Bureau of Customs and Border Protection. CBP is the federal agency with principal responsibility for inspecting cargoes, including cargo containers, that commercial ships bring into U.S. ports. Among the programs CBP has initiated to counter the terrorist threat are the Container Security Initiative (CSI) and the Customs-Trade Partnership Against Terrorism (C-TPAT). CSI is stationing U.S. inspectors at selected foreign ports to pre-screen U.S.-bound containers. In order to give inspectors the data and time they need to pre-screen containers, CBP issued a new rule requiring that information about an ocean shipment be transmitted to CBP 24 hours *before* the cargo is loaded at a foreign port onto a U.S.-bound vessel. Previously, ocean carriers did not submit this information until the ship arrived at a U.S. port.

C-TPAT, initiated in April 2002, offers importers expedited processing of cargo if they comply with CBP guidelines for securing their supply chain. Businesses that sign up for the program are required, among other things, to conduct a comprehensive self-assessment of their supply chain and submit a completed questionnaire to CBP that describes their current security practices. One of the key security controls recommended in the program is for shippers to have a "designated security officer" to supervise the container loading process as protection against the introduction of illegal material.[10] If CBP certifies an applicant, they may benefit from a reduced number of cargo inspections, thus reducing the risk of shipment delay.

Transportation Security Administration. TSA was created by the Aviation and Transportation Security Act of 2001 (P.L. 107-71) which was signed into law on November 19, 2001. TSA is responsible for the security of all modes of transportation, cargo and passenger. TSA, in conjunction with CBP, is conducting a pilot project called Operation Safe Commerce (OSC).[11] The goal of OSC is to verify the contents of sea containers at their point of loading, ensure the physical integrity of containers in transit, and track their movement through each mode of transport from origin to final destination. TSA is also field-testing a Transportation Worker Identification Credential (TWIC) for workers in all modes of transportation that will be used to control access to secure areas of cargo and passenger facilities.

ISSUES FOR CONGRESS

Addressing the Threat. A major concern for Congress is assessing whether the nation is doing enough and fast enough to deter a terrorist attack in the maritime domain. Despite the progress that has been made in strengthening port security thus far, many security officials still describe seaports as "wide open" and "very vulnerable" to terrorist attack.[12] Seaports, along with air cargo, general aviation, and mass transit, were identified in a April 2003 GAO report as the "major vulnerabilities" remaining in the nation's transportation system.[13] The GAO found that "an effective port securityenvironment may be many years away." While many agree that CSI, C-TPAT, OSC, and MDA, are sound strategies for addressing the threat, they contend that these programs represent only a framework for building a maritime security regime, and that significant gaps in security still remain. In the words of one security expert,[14]

> Right now, none of these initiatives has changed the intermodal transportation environment sufficiently to fundamentally reduce the vulnerability of the cargo container as a means of terrorism. However, all are important stepping-off points for building an effective risk management approach to container security - a foundation that simply did not exist prior to September 11, 2001.

In its oversight role, Congress is examining the effectiveness of these programs in addressing the terrorist threat, whether they are proceeding at sufficient pace, and whether enough resources are being provided to implement these and other security initiatives.

Funding Port Security. According to many, the unresolved debate over how to pay for port security is stalling efforts to improve port security. The debate is over whether port security should be paid for with federal revenues, by state and local governments, by the maritime industry, or by a cost sharing arrangement among all of the above. The Coast Guard estimates the cost of implementing the new IMO security code and the security provisions in MTSA to be approximately $1.5 billion for the first year and $7.3 billion over the succeeding decade.[15] Congress has provided over $500 million through FY2004 in direct federal grants to ports to improve their physical and operational security. This is in addition to the budgets of the Coast Guard, Bureau of Customs and Border Protection, TSA, and other federal agencies involved in port security.[16] Advocates for more spending argue that the federal grants provided to port authorities thus far is only a fraction of the amount that is needed. Skeptics of additional spending argue that taxpayers should not provide funds to large and profitable corporations to secure infrastructure that is in their own financial interest to do so.

Point of Origin Cargo Security. A major area of concern is ensuring the integrity of cargo as it begins its transit to the United States from its overseas origin. Point of origin security is necessary because inspecting cargo on the high seas is practically impossible and inspecting cargo upon its arrival at a U.S. port could be too late to prevent a terrorist event. Ensuring that the container was not stuffed with illegitimate cargo at the overseas factory, that the loaded container was not tampered with while trucked to the port of loading, and ensuring that the cargo information reported to CBP is not fraudulent are all critical challenges in supply chain security. Congress is examining the effectiveness of C-TPAT, CSI, and OSC in ensuring the integrity of U.S. bound cargo at its overseas point of origin.[17] Finding the right balance between improving cargo security to desired levels without unduly impeding the legitimate flow of commerce is a difficult issue.

Security of Ships. There is no single sovereign power that regulates international shipping. MTSA requires the Coast Guard to report on foreign-flag vessels calling at U.S. ports, specifically those vessels with murky ownership histories, and to report on actions taken to improve the transparency of vessel registration procedures (section 112). In December 2002, the International Maritime Organization (IMO), a branch of the United Nations, adopted more stringent international standards for the security of vessels and ports (titled the International Ship and Port Facility Security Code, ISPS). Congress is likely to examine the effectiveness of Coast Guard and international efforts at raising the security level of ship operators. Skeptics contend that the new IMO regulations mostly offer the illusion of increased security. They contend that "flag of convenience" countries lack the resolve to enforce these standards and that the compliance documentation is too easy to manipulate in order to appear as legitimate operators. While the United States enforces its standards when the Coast Guard selects arriving ships for boarding, their burden is greater if there is no effective international shipping regime to pre-screen substandard shipping.

Intelligence Sharing. The difficulty of detecting terrorist activity once it has entered the maritime system may point to the value of intelligence. Most acknowledge that there is just too much cargo, coming from all corners of the globe, to physically inspect each shipment thoroughly. Uncovering terrorist activity is likely to require "actionable" or precise intelligence identifying exactly which shipment to intercept. One of TSA's critical missions is to ensure that threat information gathered by other federal agencies, such as the FBI or CIA, is shared with appropriate transportation officials. The GAO reports that "in surface transportation, timely information-sharing has been hampered by the lack of standard protocols to exchange information among federal, state, and local government agencies and private entities."[18] One barrier to more effective intelligence sharing with local port authorities may be that state and local government officials do not have the required security clearances.

REFERENCES

[1] For further information on this topic, see: CRS Report RL31733, Port and Maritime Security: Background and Issues for Congress; and CRS Report RS21293, Terrorist Nuclear Attacks on Seaports: Threat and Response.

[2] Report of the Interagency Commission on Crime and Security in U.S. Seaports, Fall 2000, p. 63.

[3] For a more detailed description of the U.S. maritime system, see U.S. DOT, Maritime Admin., An Assessment of the U.S. Marine Transportation System, Sept. 1999. Available at [http://www.marad.dot.gov/].

[4] The U.S. Army Corps of Engineers' Navigation Data Center ranks U.S. ports by dollar value and tons of cargo imported and exported. See [www.iwr.usace.army.mil/ndc/].

[5] U.S. Congress, House of Representatives, Maritime Transportation Security Act of 2002, Conference Report, H.Rept. 107-777, p. 4.

[6] "The Maritime Component," Sea Power, August 2001.

[7] See William Langewiesche, "Anarchy at Sea," Atlantic Monthly, Sept. 2003, p.50. And, OECD, Ownership and Control of Ships, Maritime Transport Committee, March 2003.

[8] Admiral Thomas H. Collins, Commandant, U.S. Coast Guard, speech before the International Maritime and Port Security Conference, Singapore, Jan. 21, 2003.

[9] The Navy and the Coast Guard agree that the Coast Guard is the lead federal agency for the maritime component of homeland security, and that the Navy's role is to support the Coast Guard in areas where the Coast Guard's capabilities are limited or lacking, such as air defense or antisubmarine warfare. For more on the Coast Guard's and Navy's role in homeland security, see CRS Report RS21230, Homeland Security: Navy Operations – Background and Issues for Congress, and CRS Report RS21125, Homeland Security: Coast Guard Operations - Background and Issues for Congress.

[10] Further details of the C-TPAT program are available at [http://www.cbp.gov/xp/cgov/home.xml] (viewed 12/4/03).

[11] Federal Register, Nov. 2, 2002, p. 70110-70112.

[12] "Safe Harbors?" The Wall Street Journal, April 21, 2003, p. B1. Also, Maarten van de Voort and Kevin A. O'Brien, et. al., Seacurity, RAND Europe, 2003.
[13] GAO, Transportation Security, Post September 11th Initiatives and Long-Term Challenges, April 1, 2003, GAO-03-616T.
[14] Stephen Flynn, "On The Record," Government Executive Magazine, October 1, 2003.
[15] See Federal Register, October 22, 2003 vol. 68, no. 204, p. 60464.
[16] See CRS Report RL32061, Border and Transportation Security: Budget for FY2003 and FY2004.
[17] See Senate Governmental Affairs Committee, Letter to Under Secretary for Border and Transportation Security, dated October 28, 2003, regarding point of origin security measures. Available at [http://govt-aff.senate.gov/], viewed on 11/10/03. See also, GAO, Container Security: Expansion of Key Customs Programs Will Require Greater Attention to Critical Success Factors, July 2003, GAO-03-770.
[18] GAO, Transportation Security, Post-September 11th Initiatives and Long-Term Challenges, April 1, 2003, GAO-03-616T.

In: Port and Maritime Security ISBN 1-59454-726-2
Editor: Jonathon P. Vesky © 2008 Nova Science Publishers, Inc.

Chapter 4

PORT AND MARITIME SECURITY: POTENTIAL FOR TERRORIST NUCLEAR ATTACK USING OIL TANKERS[*]

Jonathan Medalia

ABSTRACT

While much attention has been focused on threats to maritime security posed by cargo container ships, terrorists could also attempt to use oil tankers to stage an attack. If they were able to place an atomic bomb in a tanker and detonate it in a U.S. port, they would cause massive destruction and might halt crude oil shipments worldwide for some time. Detecting a bomb in a tanker would be difficult. Congress may consider various options to address this threat.

INTRODUCTION

The terrorist attacks of September 11, 2001, heightened interest in port and maritime security.[1] Much of this interest has focused on cargo

---

[*] From CRS Report RS21997; December 7 2004

container ships because of concern that terrorists could use containers to transport weapons into the United States, yet only a small fraction of the millions of cargo containers entering the country each year is inspected. Some observers fear that a container-borne atomic bomb detonated in a U.S. port could wreak economic as well as physical havoc. Robert Bonner, the head of Customs and Border Protection (CBP) within the Department of Homeland Security (DHS), has argued that such an attack would lead to a halt to container traffic worldwide for some time, bringing the world economy to its knees. Stephen Flynn, a retired Coast Guard commander and an expert on maritime security at the Council on Foreign Relations, holds a similar view.[2]

While container ships accounted for 30.5% of vessel calls to U.S. ports in 2003, other ships carried crude oil (13.2%), petroleum products (19.3%), bulk cargo (18.1%), and cars and trucks (9.1%).[3] These ships merit attention as well because terrorists will look for the weak link. The 9/11 Commission stressed the importance of a balanced approach to maritime security.[4] To this end, this report focuses on the threat of a terrorist nuclear attack using oil tanker ships. This threat is of particular interest because the Middle East is the chief source of anti-U.S. terrorism.

BACKGROUND

Oil Shipments from the Middle East. Crude oil and other petroleum products account for almost all export earnings of many Middle Eastern nations.[5] In turn, 25.6% of net U.S. crude oil imports in July 2004 came from the Middle East.[6] Crude oil from the Middle East went to 30 U.S. ports in 2003. Those handling the most oil were Blaine, WA; El Segundo, Long Beach, Los Angeles, and Richmond, CA; Corpus Christi, Freeport, Galveston, Houston, Port Arthur, and Texas City, TX; Baton Rouge, Gramercy, Lake Charles, Morgan City, and New Orleans, LA; Pascagoula, MS; Mobile, AL; Wilmington, DE; and Paulsboro, NJ.[7]

Crude oil from the Middle East is typically shipped to the United States in supertankers — Very Large Crude Carriers (VLCCs) and Ultra Large Crude Carriers (ULCCs). Their size is measured in deadweight tons (DWT), the weight of the stores, fuel, and cargo they can carry. One DWT is 2,240 lb. While definitions vary slightly, VLCCs can carry about

200,000 to 300,000 DWT and ULCCs can carry more than 300,000 DWT. A representative ULCC was 60 meters wide and 350 meters long, and had a draft (depth below the waterline) of 22 meters. They are the largest ships ever built. The interior of a tanker is divided into multiple storage tanks.

Both the Coast Guard and the Navy state that they do not have responsibility for, or authority over, security of foreign-flagged vessels at foreign ports.[8] Nor do other American forces. Security of foreign ports rests with foreign governments.

Staging a Terrorist Nuclear Attack Using Tankers. The simplest type of atomic bomb, and by far the easiest to fabricate, is a gun-assembly bomb, in which one mass of uranium highly enriched in the fissile isotope 235 (highly enriched uranium, or HEU) is shot down a tube into another mass of HEU, forming a critical mass and causing a nuclear explosion. The Hiroshima bomb was of this type; its designers had such confidence in the design that it was not tested before use. This bomb had an explosive yield of 15 kilotons (equivalent to 15,000 tons of TNT). Excluding the bomb's outer casing, fins, and fuses, this device was 6 feet long and about 6 inches in diameter, and weighed about 1,000 pounds.[9] Some items loaded onto large cargo ships are of similar or greater size and weight. It might be possible to make a gun-assembly bomb lighter, or to obtain a more advanced, lightweight "suitcase bomb."

To stage a nuclear attack using a tanker, terrorists would need to acquire a nuclear device[10] and smuggle it (or key components) onto the ship. Their ability to accomplish this latter task would likely depend on their ability to infiltrate, bribe, or otherwise work around local security; on the reliability of security personnel in oil-exporting countries such as Saudi Arabia, Kuwait, and Algeria; and on the reliability of the ship's officers and crew. Terrorists might seek to place a nuclear device inside one of a tanker's oil tanks, which would require sealing and cushioning the bomb and possibly attaching it to the tank wall; or in a dry space on the ship; or in a blister attached to the ship underwater. Remotely detonating a bomb inside an oil tank or underwater might be difficult: it might not be possible to attach wires leading out to dry spaces, or to send an electromagnetic signal (e.g., a cell phone call) through water or oil to the bomb. Detonating the bomb with a timer would run the risk of the ship not being at the target at the specified time. Overcoming these challenges might be within the ability of a terrorist group resourceful enough to acquire an atomic bomb. Terrorists might also smuggle a bomb onto a ship at sea, as discussed later.

Potential Targets. Terrorists could be expected to target a port that handled a large volume of oil and other goods and that had a densely-populated area that tankers passed on their way through a harbor to an unloading terminal. Various cities worldwide meet these criteria. If terrorists sought major economic damage while minimizing loss of life, they might try to target the Louisiana Offshore Oil Port, or LOOP, the only U.S. deepwater oil port that can handle fully loaded supertankers. LOOP, 18 miles off the Louisiana coast, currently handles about 10% of U.S. crude oil imports. The Panama Canal might be another potential economic target.

Detecting an Atomic Bomb in a Tanker. Some technical approaches for detecting atomic bombs in a tanker would fail, especially for a bomb inside an oil tank. Gamma rays, essentially high-energy x-rays, can be used to create x-ray-type pictures of the contents of cargo containers, but a tanker's sheer mass of oil and steel would prevent any gamma rays from traveling the width of a tanker. Neutrons may also be used to detect fissile material; neutrons of the appropriate energy level cause such material to fission, producing neutrons and gamma rays that can be detected. The hydrogen and carbon atoms of crude oil, however, would block neutrons from penetrating. Another possible approach, muon detection, might work if daunting technical approaches could be overcome.[11] Other candidate techniques include chemical sampling of oil for traces of extraneous material, and preparing an acoustic profile of a ship when known to be "clean" to compare with a profile taken as the ship nears port. The vast amount of oil in a supertanker works against the former technique; the complex configuration of tanks on a tanker works against the latter.

Securing Tankers. The difficulty of detecting a bomb aboard a tanker underscores the importance of preventing bombs from being placed aboard tankers. Securing tankers at loading terminals would likely involve setting and enforcing a security perimeter (including underwater), and instituting measures to ensure personnel reliability. Items brought on board a ship would have to be screened. A National Nuclear Security Administration program, "Second Line of Defense," screens people and baggage for fissile material; similar technology might be used to secure tankers.

Securing tankers in port might not be adequate if terrorists could smuggle a bomb onto a ship at sea. It may be possible to improve security by using surveillance aircraft or satellites. Security may be a greater issue as tankers slow to navigate straits or approach port. Several issues arise: (1) Would shippers let crew spend time to upgrade security beyond current levels? VLCCs have small crews, perhaps 40 people, who may have no time for added tasks. (2) If intelligence data indicated a plot to board a tanker at sea to place a bomb, could a warning be passed without compromising U.S. intelligence capabilities? (3) This scenario would require the connivance of the entire crew, or silencing those who opposed the plot. Screening for personnel reliability may be the only defense against this prospect.

POTENTIAL OVERSIGHT QUESTIONS AND OPTIONS FOR CONGRESS

Oversight Questions. Possible oversight questions include the following:

- What is the Administration's view on the potential for terrorists to use an oil tanker as a vehicle for a nuclear attack? To what extent has the Administration considered this threat in planning for port and maritime security?
- If considered a serious threat, what measures is the Administration implementing to respond to it? When will they be in place? How much funding is programmed for them over the next few years? Which areas of detection technology may merit development?
- Which executive branch office has overall responsibility for examining or addressing this potential threat? What other executive offices have responsibilities in this area? Is there adequate coordination among them?

Potential Options. Congress might consider options such as the following to further explore the threat discussed in this report. If Congress found the threat credible, it could:

- **Clarify federal responsibility for tanker security** by requiring a lead federal agency for tanker security and making more explicit the responsibilities of various federal agencies involved in tanker security.
- **Create a Tanker Security Initiative (TSI)** analogous to the Container Security Initiative for improving containerized cargo security.[12] TSI might set security standards for tankers that transport oil to U.S. ports, and for the ports where they load. Tankers not meeting the standards, or that come from ports not meeting the standards, could be denied entry to U.S. ports. Establishing such a regime would undoubtedly require negotiations with other countries.
- **Ensure that tankers are a focus of maritime domain awareness,** which refers to surveillance and communication systems that would permit U.S. officials to have a comprehensive understanding at any given moment of the location and identity of ships at sea.[13]
- **Assure sufficient U.S. intelligence assets are focused on the threat** and possible indications of preparations for such an attack. Terrorists seeking to acquire or build a bomb and smuggle it onto a tanker would need to go through certain steps. Similarly, a terrorist bomb placed inside a tank of crude oil might have certain signatures, such as a way to detonate the bomb. The Intelligence Community could analyze such steps and signatures, and be alert to signs of the most critical ones.

- **Determine whether funding is adequate for technologies** that hold some prospect of detecting an atomic bomb aboard a tanker.
- **Keep oil tankers away from U.S. ports** by promoting the construction of more offshore ports like LOOP.
- **Improve international cooperation.** Existing international agreements and organizations that might focus on tanker security include agreements for countering narcotics, crime, and piracy; the International Maritime Organization, shipping associations, and Interpol; and the International Ship and Port Facility Security Code. These efforts could supplement the Proliferation Security Initiative (PSI), a multilateral effort for interdicting ships at sea that are suspected of carrying weapons of mass destruction.
- Ships available for PSI missions might respond to indications of tanker security problems at sea.[14] The United States could pursue increased bilateral cooperation with oil-exporting states and countries under whose flags tankers are registered. Potential measures include improved perimeter security at oil-loading terminals and more rigorous background screening and training of port workers and tanker crew members.

Should Congress conclude that proactive steps should be taken in this area, the issues of who should pay and how funds should be collected would arise. Costs could be covered by general revenues. Alternatives would be to charge a fee on ships landing oil in the United States or to impose a tax on crude oil or petroleum products consumed in the United States.

REFERENCES

[1] For discussions, see CRS Report RL31733, Port and Maritime Security: Background and Issues for Congress, by John Frittelli; and CRS Report RS21293, Terrorist Nuclear Attacks on Seaports: Threat and Response, by Jonathan Medalia.

[2] U.S. Department of the Treasury. "U.S. Customs Commissioner Robert Bonner, Speech Before the Center for Strategic and International Studies," Washington, D.C., January 17, 2002; and Stephen Flynn, America the Vulnerable: How Our Government Is Failing to Protect Us from Terrorism (New York: HarperCollins, 2004) p. 83.

[3] U.S. Department of Transportation, Maritime Administration, Vessel Calls at U.S. Ports, 2003, p. 4.

[4] U.S. National Commission on Terrorist Attacks upon the United States, The 9/11 Commission Report, Authorized edition (New York: Norton, 2004) p. 391.

[5] The figures are 90-95% for Saudi Arabia and 95% for Kuwait (source: U.S. Department of Energy, Energy Information Administration, Country Analysis Briefs) and roughly 85% for Qatar (source: U.S. Central Intelligence Agency, The World Factbook).

[6] U.S. Department of Energy, Energy Information Administration, "Table 3.7: United States —Oil Imports (Most Recent 12 Months)" for August 2003-July 2004.

[7] U.S. Department of Energy, Energy Information Administration, Petroleum Data Publications, "Company Level Imports," The American Petroleum Institute aggregated the port and monthly data from these tables for CRS.

[8] Source: Discussions with Navy and Coast Guard officers, November 2004.

[9] Thomas Cochran, William Arkin, and Milton Hoenig, Nuclear Weapons Databook, volume I: U.S. Nuclear Forces and Capabilities, (Cambridge, MA: Ballinger, 1984) p. 32.

[10] CRS Report RL32595, Nuclear Terrorism: A Brief Review of Threats and Responses, by Jonathan Medalia, discusses how terrorists might acquire a nuclear device.

[11] Muons are subatomic particles produced when cosmic rays from space strike atoms in the upper atmosphere. Some 10,000 muons per minute strike each square meter of Earth. They can penetrate many meters of rock. Their path is bent slightly in proportion to the density and atomic number (number of protons in the nucleus) of the material. Los Alamos National Laboratory has conducted experiments to determine if muons can be used to detect fissile material in cargo containers. The technique involves placing a flat-plate detector above and below the container to measure how much the paths of individual muons are bent. Detectors would have to be scaled up immensely to go from a container to a VLCC. Detection could be time-consuming: the level of detail increases with number of muons, which increases with time. See Brian Fishbine, "Muon Radiography: Detecting Nuclear Contraband," Los Alamos Research Quarterly, Spring 2003.

[12] For more on the Container Security Initiative, see CRS Report RL31733, op cit, p. 12-13.

[13] For more on maritime domain awareness, see CRS Report RL31733, op cit, p. 12.

[14] For more on PSI, see CRS Report RS21881, Proliferation Security Initiative (PSI), by Sharon Squassoni.

INDEX

#

9/11 Commission, 7, 9, 13, 30, 37, 40, 54, 60

A

access, 3, 6, 24, 33, 34, 47
accessibility, ix, 43
accidents, 16
accounting, 15, 25
administration, ix, 12, 31
aging, 23
agricultural, 15
aircraft, 22, 23, 57
airports, 28, 29, 33
al Qaeda, 19, 38, 39
Algeria, 55
allies, 4
American Association for the Advancement of Science, 9
analysts, 16
appropriations, 29
Arabia, 55, 60
Army Corps of Engineers, 37, 50
assessment, 5, 24, 46
assets, 30, 58
atmosphere, 61
atoms, 56, 61

attacks, vii, viii, ix, 6, 11, 12, 17, 18, 22, 32, 43, 44, 53
attention, vii, viii, ix, 11, 13, 14, 45, 53, 54
Attorney General, 35
authority, 21, 26, 34, 45, 55
automakers, 14
availability, 3
aviation, 7, 13, 27, 47
awareness, vii, viii, 11, 13, 23, 58, 61

B

background information, 12
baggage, 56
barges, 14
basic services, 21
benchmarks, 33
benefits, 16, 30
Bin Laden, Osama, 39
biological weapons, 17
bomb, viii, ix, 1, 2, 3, 4, 5, 6, 8, 18, 24, 39, 53, 54, 55, 56, 57, 58, 59
bonds, 21
Brussels, 25
Bulgaria, 4, 8
Bureau of Customs and Border Protection, vii, viii, 7, 9, 12, 21, 22, 23, 29, 45, 46, 48

bypass, 2

C

California, 14
Canada, 38
carbon atoms, 56
cargo, vii, viii, ix, 2, 4, 5, 6, 7, 9, 11, 12, 13, 14, 15, 16, 17, 18, 19, 20, 22, 23, 24, 25, 26, 27, 28, 29, 31, 34, 35, 36, 37, 38, 43, 44, 45, 46, 47, 48, 49, 50, 53, 54, 55, 56, 58, 61
Caribbean, 36
carrier, 20, 38
cell, 55
Central Intelligence Agency (CIA), 49, 60
channels, 14, 21, 44
chemical, 1, 17, 19, 56
Chinese, 3
civilian, 16, 22
Coast Guard, vii, viii, ix, 9, 12, 13, 20, 21, 22, 23, 25, 26, 28, 29, 31, 32, 37, 39, 41, 45, 46, 48, 49, 50, 54, 55, 60
Cold War, 7
combat, 2
commerce, 2, 13, 14, 16, 21, 23, 35, 44, 45, 49
commercial, 7, 13, 14, 16, 17, 22, 23, 33, 44, 46
Committee on Homeland Security, 41
Committee on the Judiciary, 8, 36
commodity, 33
communication systems, 58
community, 34
complexity, 19
compliance, 32, 49
components, 15, 17, 20, 55
confidence, 3, 55
configuration, 56
Congress, vii, viii, ix, x, 1, 7, 11, 12, 13, 25, 26, 27, 28, 29, 30, 31, 32, 33, 35, 37, 38, 39, 43, 44, 47, 48, 49, 50, 53, 57, 58, 59, 60

consensus, 32
construction, 59
consumer goods, 14
Container Security Initiative (CSI), vii, ix, 4, 12, 23, 28, 31, 36, 41, 46, 47, 48, 58, 61
container ships, vii, viii, 11, 14, 45
control, 2, 16, 17, 19, 24, 35, 47
conversion, 4
conviction, 34
corporations, 29, 48
cosmic rays, 61
cost-effective, 4, 30
costs, 2, 15, 16, 26, 30
credentials, 33, 34
credibility, 31
crime, 35, 59
crude oil, ix, 14, 38, 53, 54, 56, 58, 59
C-TPAT, vii, ix, 12, 23, 24, 28, 31, 35, 41, 46, 47, 48, 50
curriculum, 25
customers, 19, 33
Customs and Border Protection (CBP), vii, viii, ix, 2, 4, 5, 6, 7, 9, 12, 13, 15, 16, 20, 21, 22, 23, 24, 25, 26, 28, 29, 31, 35, 37, 45, 46, 47, 48, 54
Customs Service, 22, 25, 38
cutters, 22

D

data collection, 35
database, 36
death(s), 13, 17, 44
decisions, 30
defense, 3, 5, 7, 32, 39, 50, 57
Delaware, 21
demand, 17, 30
density, 61
Department of Defense (DOD), 4, 16, 38
Department of Energy (DOE), 4, 60
Department of Homeland Security (DHS), 4, 6, 7, 9, 21, 25, 26, 27, 30, 34, 36, 40, 45, 54

Department of Justice, 22
Department of Transportation (DOT), 5, 9, 22, 26, 37, 38, 39, 50, 60
designers, 55
destruction, ix, 1, 6, 13, 18, 20, 44, 53, 59
detection, 4, 6, 8, 36, 56, 57
developing countries, 30
discharges, 38
discrimination, 38
dispersion, 39
distribution, 15
diversity, 33
draft, 25, 55
drugs, 20
duplication, 34
duties, 36

E

earnings, 54
economic damages, 29
economic problem, 2
economy, viii, 1, 2, 13, 15, 16, 45, 54
Egypt, 38
Egyptian, 18
electric power, 7
electromagnetic, 55
electronic, 5, 16, 25, 26
emergency preparedness, 7
energy, 56
Energy Information Administration, 60
environment, 20, 23, 24, 27, 28, 35, 45, 48
environmental, 17
equipment, 4, 6, 8, 16, 18, 36
EU, 38
Europe, 51
expenditures, 13
expert(s), ix, 3, 13, 16, 17, 19, 20, 28, 30, 32, 35, 43, 44, 47, 54
expertise, 4
exporter, 19, 20
exports, 15

F

fabricate, 1, 55
failure, 7, 20
false alarms, 24
farm, 38
FBI, 2, 8, 20, 44, 49
fear, 2, 3, 54
federal funds, 29
federal government, 21, 27, 29
federal grants, 7, 29, 48
Federal Register, 39, 40, 50, 51
fee(s), 26, 29, 30, 36, 40, 59
feet, 3, 14, 45, 55
finance, 19, 21, 26, 29
financial support, 30
fires, 2
firms, 14, 44
fishing, 18
fission, 3, 56
flow, 16, 23, 45, 49
forensic, 6
freight, 19
fuel, 17, 54
funding, 26, 28, 29, 30, 36, 57, 59
funds, viii, 1, 7, 21, 26, 27, 29, 30, 48, 59

G

Gamma, 56
gamma rays, 56
global economy, viii, 1, 2, 13, 16
government, 4, 5, 21, 25, 27, 29, 34, 35, 44, 48, 49, 55
grants, 4, 7, 26, 29, 36, 48
greed, 28
gross domestic product (GDP), 15, 16, 45
groups, 2, 3
guidelines, 24, 46

H

harm, 7, 13
Harvard, 8
hazardous materials, 34
head, 54
high-risk, 4
Hiroshima, 2, 3, 55
homeland security, vii, viii, ix, 5, 7, 8, 9, 11, 12, 21, 22, 25, 33, 36, 39, 40, 41, 43, 45, 50, 54
host, ix, 4, 12, 31
house, 8, 25, 35, 37, 50
hydrogen, 56

I

identification, 6, 27
identity, 19, 31, 58
illusion, 32, 49
immigration, 22
implementation, 26
imports, 14, 54, 56
incidence, 20
incidents, 9, 40
India, 3
indigenous, 3
industry, 5, 22, 29, 32, 34, 48
infrastructure, 14, 21, 29, 30, 33, 44, 48
inspection(s), 8, 24, 26, 28, 32, 39, 47
inspectors, vii, ix, 12, 23, 32, 36, 45, 46
institutions, 25
insurance, 16
integration, 5
integrity, 16, 19, 24, 28, 31, 47, 48
intelligence, viii, 1, 2, 5, 6, 19, 23, 26, 34, 49, 57, 58
Intelligence Community, 58
Intelligence Reform and Terrorism Prevention Act, 13, 27
international, viii, 1, 5, 9, 15, 23, 28, 31, 32, 35, 49, 59

International Atomic Energy Agency (IAEA), 4, 8
international standards, 32, 49
international trade, 15, 32
interstate, 21
inventories, 3, 15, 16
Investigations, 41
Iran, 3
isotope, 3, 55

J

jobs, 34
judiciary, 8, 36
jurisdiction, 21

K

killing, 18
knees, 54
Korea, 3
Kuwait, 55, 60

L

labor, 15, 34
land, ix, 17, 43
law, 13, 16, 21, 25, 26, 28, 44, 45, 47
law enforcement, 21, 45
lawyers, 38
lead, 5, 6, 21, 39, 45, 50, 54, 58
leadership, 28
legislation, 13, 26, 27, 29
Libya, 3, 4, 9
links, 19
liquefied natural gas, 17
literature, 3
local government, 21, 29, 35, 48, 49
location, 24, 58
location information, 24
logistics, 16
Los Angeles, 54
Louisiana, 56

Index

M

major cities, 2
management, 15, 16, 23, 28, 48
mandates, 5, 9, 25
MARAD, 21, 22, 25
marine environment, 20, 23, 35, 45
Maritime Administration, 21, 22, 25, 36, 37, 39, 60
Maritime Transportation Security Act, viii, ix, 5, 12, 13, 22, 25, 37, 43, 44, 46, 50
MCP, 4
measures, iv, viii, ix, 5, 12, 25, 28, 30, 31, 33, 34, 51, 56, 57, 59
Mediterranean, 18
Middle East, 54
military, 16, 17
Millender-McDonald, 35
missiles, 2
missions, 49, 59
modernization, 38
money, 15, 19
movement, 18, 24, 47
muon(s), 56, 61

N

narcotic(s), 16, 59
nation, ix, 4, 15, 21, 27, 43, 45, 47
National Research Council, 3, 8
national security, 16
natural, 6, 16, 17
natural disasters, 16
natural gas, 17
network, 32, 34
neutrons, 56
New Jersey, 21
New Orleans, 54
New York, 7, 8, 9, 21, 37, 40, 60
New York Times, 8, 9
NOA, vii, viii, 12, 23, 46
North America, 15, 45
North Korea, 3
Notice of Arrival, vii, viii, 12, 23, 46
nuclear material, viii, 1, 3, 6, 26
nuclear program, 3
nuclear weapons, 1, 2, 3, 4, 5, 6, 7, 32
nucleus, 61

O

obligation, 21
offshore oil, 38
oil, ix, 14, 17, 18, 38, 53, 54, 55, 56, 57, 58, 59
oil spill, 18
operator, 21
Organization for Economic Cooperation and Development (OECD), 19, 37, 38, 50
organizations, 59
oversight, vii, viii, 11, 13, 28, 35, 48, 57
ownership, 19, 21, 31, 44, 49

P

Pacific, 19
Pakistan, 3, 8
Pakistani, 3
Panama, 56
particles, 61
partnership, 34
passenger, vii, viii, 11, 14, 22, 24, 44, 47
PATRIOT Act, 34
penalties, 36
performance, 27
permit, 15, 58
personal, 18, 38
petroleum, 60
petroleum products, 54, 59
Philadelphia, 7
pipelines, 7
piracy, 19, 59
planning, 16, 22, 27, 57
plants, 7

plutonium, 3
point of origin, 31, 32, 41, 49, 51
police, 21
policymakers, 29, 30, 34, 35
ports, vii, viii, ix, 1, 2, 4, 5, 6, 7, 11, 12, 13, 14, 15, 16, 17, 18, 20, 21, 22, 23, 26, 29, 30, 31, 33, 34, 37, 38, 40, 43, 44, 46, 48, 49, 50, 54, 55, 58, 59
power, 7, 31, 49
power plants, 7
preparedness, 7
President Bush, 4, 5
priorities, 30
private sector, 21, 35
probability, 6
procedures, 25, 31, 49
productivity, 16
profits, 35
program, vii, ix, 5, 12, 23, 24, 26, 28, 31, 35, 39, 46, 50, 56
property, 2, 35
protocols, 35, 49
protons, 61
public, 13, 21, 23
public safety, 13

Q

Qatar, 60
questionnaire, 24, 46

R

R&D, 5, 6, 9
radiation, 4, 6, 36
radiological, 1, 17, 24, 39
radiological dispersion device, 39
radius, 6
rail, 2, 7, 14, 15, 20
random, 16, 36
range, 2, 6, 8
recovery, 5, 7
recreational, 18

refineries, 17
regional, 21, 26
regulations, 14, 19, 23, 25, 26, 32, 33, 34, 41, 45, 49
reliability, 55, 56, 57
repair, 18, 34
residential, 5
resources, ix, 7, 28, 30, 33, 43, 48
revenue, 21
risk, vii, viii, 4, 8, 12, 16, 23, 24, 28, 34, 45, 47, 48, 55
risk management, 28, 48
River Po, 21
river ports, vii, viii, 11, 14, 44
Rome, 38
Russia, 2, 3, 4, 6, 8

S

safeguards, 4
safety, 13, 22, 46
sampling, 56
satellite, 18
Saudi Arabia, 55, 60
sea containers, 47
seals, 16, 27
search(ing), 4, 6, 20
Secretary General, 30
Secretary of Homeland Security, 33
security, vii, viii, ix, 3, 4, 5, 7, 11, 12, 13, 14, 16, 20, 21, 22, 23, 24, 25, 26, 27, 28, 29, 30, 31, 32, 33, 34, 35, 36, 39, 40, 41, 43, 44, 45, 46, 47, 48, 49, 50, 51, 53, 54, 55, 56, 57, 58, 59
Security Council, 20
seizure, 18
self-assessment, 24, 46
senate, 8, 25, 36, 41, 51
sensors, 5, 16, 26
September 11, vii, viii, ix, 8, 11, 12, 22, 28, 32, 40, 41, 43, 44, 48, 51, 53
series, 23
sharing, 29, 35, 48, 49

Index

shipping, 7, 13, 15, 17, 20, 27, 31, 32, 36, 38, 49, 59
shores, 4
sign(s), 24, 46, 58
Singapore, 50
sites, 3
skills, 3, 8
smuggling, 6, 16, 20
Southeast Asia, 19
species, 16
specificity, 13, 26
speech, 50
speed, 15, 16, 24
standards, viii, ix, 5, 12, 25, 27, 32, 33, 43, 49, 58
steel, 56
storage, 2, 55
strategic, 6, 16, 30
strategies, 28, 47
suppliers, 15, 25
supply, viii, ix, 5, 12, 20, 24, 26, 31, 46, 48
supply chain, viii, ix, 5, 12, 20, 24, 26, 31, 46, 48
surveillance, 57, 58
systems, 5, 26, 58

T

tankers, ix, 53, 56, 57, 58, 59
tanks, 55, 56
targets, viii, 1, 2, 7
taxpayers, 29, 48
technology, viii, 1, 6, 30, 36, 56, 57
terminals, vii, viii, 11, 14, 26, 44, 56, 59
terrorism, 4, 13, 18, 19, 20, 24, 27, 28, 34, 44, 48, 54
terrorist(s), vii, viii, ix, 1, 2, 3, 4, 5, 6, 7, 8, 11, 12, 13, 16, 17, 18, 19, 20, 21, 22, 23, 27, 28, 31, 32, 33, 34, 35, 43, 44, 45, 46, 47, 48, 49, 53, 54, 55, 56, 58
terrorist attack, vii, viii, ix, 2, 4, 5, 7, 11, 12, 13, 16, 18, 22, 27, 32, 33, 43, 44, 47, 53
terrorist groups, 2, 3
Texas, 54
theft, 16, 20, 29
threat(s), viii, ix, x, 3, 12, 13, 16, 17, 18, 20, 22, 23, 27, 28, 44, 45, 46, 47, 48, 49, 53, 54, 57, 58
time, x, 6, 15, 17, 23, 24, 33, 35, 46, 53, 54, 55, 57, 61
timing, vii, ix, 12, 23, 45
toys, 14
tracking, 16, 23, 24
trade, 2, 7, 14, 15, 16, 17, 18, 25, 30, 32, 34, 40, 44, 45
Trade Act, 5, 9, 26
trade agreement, 32
trading, 15
traffic, 14, 17, 23, 44, 54
training, 25, 59
transmission, 26
transparency, 19, 31, 44, 49
transport, 5, 24, 47, 54, 58
transportation, vii, viii, 5, 7, 11, 13, 14, 15, 16, 20, 21, 22, 24, 25, 26, 27, 28, 30, 32, 33, 34, 35, 44, 45, 47, 48, 49
transportation security, 5, 13, 26, 33
Transportation Security Administration (TSA), 9, 21, 22, 24, 25, 29, 30, 34, 45, 47, 48
treasury, 8, 38, 60
trucks, 15, 18, 54
trust, 21, 29, 35
trust fund, 21, 29
trustworthiness, 20, 33

U

U.S. Department of the Treasury, 38, 60
U.S. economy, 15, 45
U.S. military, 17
uniform, 33
United Nations, 37, 49

United States, iv, viii, 1, 2, 4, 5, 6, 9, 13, 14, 15, 16, 17, 18, 20, 23, 26, 27, 31, 32, 37, 40, 44, 45, 48, 49, 54, 59, 60
universities, 5
uranium, 3, 4, 6, 55
urban areas, 18
users, 30

V

vessels, 5, 14, 16, 19, 22, 23, 26, 31, 44, 46, 49, 55
visible, 4
vulnerability, vii, viii, 2, 3, 5, 11, 13, 20, 27, 28, 30, 44, 48

W

Wall Street Journal, 40, 51
war, 13, 20
war on terror, 13
warfare, 39, 50
Washington, 8, 9, 38, 39, 60
water, ix, 43, 55
waterways, 22, 46
weapons, 1, 2, 3, 4, 5, 6, 7, 8, 13, 17, 18, 32, 44, 54, 59
weapons of mass destruction (WMD), 1, 4, 6, 13, 44, 59
wires, 55
workers, 7, 24, 28, 33, 34, 47, 59
World War, vii, viii, 12, 22
worry, 35, 44

X

x-ray(s), 15, 56

Y

Yemen, 18
yield, 2, 6, 55